# Ascending Peculiarity

# Ascending Peculiarity

# Edward Gorey on Edward Gorey

INTERVIEWS SELECTED AND EDITED

BY KAREN WILKIN

HARCOURT, INC.

NEW YORK • SAN DIEGO • LONDON

B
GOREY

www.harcourt.com

Library of Congress Cataloging-in-Publication Data
Gorey, Edward, 1925–2000
Ascending peculiarity: Edward Gorey on Edward Gorey: interviews / selected and
edited by Karen Wilkin—1st ed.
p.   cm.
Includes bibliographical references and index.
ISBN 0-15-100504-4
1. Gorey, Edward, 1925—Interviews. 2. Artists—United States—Interviews.
3. Authors—United States—Interviews. I. Title: Edward Gorey on Edward Gorey
II. Wilkin, Karen. III. Title.

NX512.G67 A35 2001
700'.92—dc21
[B]   2001024101

Text set in Granjon

Designed by BTDnyc

First Edition
K J I H G F E D C B A

Printed in the United States of America

# Contents

# Edward Gorey: An Introduction

"I just kind of conjured them up
out of my subconscious
and put them in order
of ascending peculiarity."

— EDWARD GOREY

The first known request for an interview with Edward St. John Gorey was telegraphed to his mother the day after his birth on February 22, 1925: "Hooray! I'm proud of you. Have designs on your young son already. Use your influence so that I can get an interview with him soon." Gorey's response is not recorded, but in later life he is famously reported to have met similar proposals with "on pain of death," "absolutely not," and "I really haven't anything to say." "Anyway, the facts of my life are so few, tedious, and irrelevant to anything else, there is no point in going into them," he told one writer. "And as far as my work is concerned, I've never given it any thought except what was necessary to doing it, so I don't really even know what it is like, much less what it is about," he told another.

Yet the notoriously diffident Gorey was also unfailingly generous and accommodating to would-be interviewers—as well as to just about everyone else, including people making outrageous demands on his time. Asked in one interview what he would choose, if he could change one thing about himself, he opted for the ability to say no. Even "on pain of death" was not an unqualified refusal. Between 1973 and 1999 this reluctant subject granted more than seventy interviews in the United States, Great Britain, and Germany. And Gorey, always a gracious and amiable companion, and a voluble talker once he got going, frequently seems to have enjoyed or, at least, to have been interested in the process.

Together, this collection of more than a quarter century of interviews constitutes a loosely sketched self-portrait, an informal, freewheeling autobiography in Gorey's own words. The facts of his life, sometimes embellished, compressed, or edited for literary effect, gradually emerge so that through an accumulation of offhand allusions to Gorey's Chicago childhood, his Harvard years, and his early days in New York, we begin to understand how the author and illustrator of those uncanny little books was formed. Not that Gorey was particularly forthright. Since he was always less ready to talk about himself than to discuss the things that engaged him most passionately—which included everything from the ballets of George Balanchine to cats, from classical Japanese literature to television sit-coms, and from obscure silent films to yard sales, all of it embraced with relish and filtered through a penetrating intelligence—the interviews can perhaps most accurately be described as a catalogue of Gorey's eclectic obsessions and tastes, a record of what one interviewer called his "cultural voraciousness." What rapidly becomes clear is that Gorey's curiosity was dazzlingly wide-ranging, that his breadth of knowledge was astonishing. He had an insatiable appetite for both high and low culture, and a connoisseur's enthusiasm not only for arcane objects but for arcane ideas—"a man of enormous erudition," as one writer described him.

Routine or ill-informed questions bored him, although he would answer politely, gently correcting errors of fact and interpretation, almost without appearing to do so. But when an interviewer had deep, specialized knowledge of something Gorey was obsessed by, then he held nothing back. With a certain amount of informed encouragement, he would unselfconsciously make use of his vast store of information so that the slightly skewed subtlety and complexity of his thinking became immediately apparent. When interviewers hadn't done their home-work, Gorey didn't volunteer a great deal. Since no one, for example, seems ever to have asked him about music, even though it was a very large part of his life, he never offered any opinions on the subject, other than to mention that he listened to Mozart, Schubert, and Bach, but played no musical instrument.

If Gorey found his questioner sympathetic, he might offer a new biographical fragment. In an interview published in *Esquire* in 1974, Gorey told Alexander Theroux: "My great-grandmother—my mother's father's mother—is the single person, I guess, from whom I inherited my, well, talent. Or whatever you want to call it. Helen St. John Garvey was her name. She supported the family in the mid-nineteenth century by, oh, illustrating greeting cards and writing mottoes." Theroux noted that Helen St. John Garvey's diploma and some of her watercolors hung directly over Gorey's desk in Barnstable. When we read such a conver-sation, it's easy to be (perhaps rightly) convinced that we are seeing the "real" Gorey: thoughtful, deliciously verbal, serious, astonishingly informed, friendly, although even here there is a suggestion that only a fraction of a carefully constructed persona is being revealed.

Despite his repeated protestations about having nothing to say, the extant interviews make it clear that Gorey was not only fascinating and articulate, but also utterly charming, a delight to spend time with—once common ground was established. Yet it is equally plain that, his charm, wit, and politeness notwithstanding, Gorey was not only essentially guarded and self-protective, but also possessed of an edge, an acute "take no prisoners" critical sense. "The personality is playful, amusing, evasive," Richard Dyer noted in a 1984 interview for the *Boston Globe*. "Gorey is opinionated, and even, at times, vicious," wrote Stephen Schiff in a *New Yorker* profile in 1992, "but he's almost childishly unaware that anyone might find what he says objectionable; one has the impression that if he actually discovered himself giving offense, the remorse would overwhelm him." In this context, however, it's useful to keep in mind that the accommodating, amiable Gorey had carefully designed a life for himself that ensured his privacy and allowed him long periods of uninterrupted solitude. "There have been winters up here when I hardly saw anyone," he told a writer who visited him on Cape Cod, "and I don't remember feeling particularly bothered by it."

Then, of course, there was Gorey's appearance—"half bongo-drum beatnik, half fin-de-siècle dandy," as Schiff described him. Everyone who met Gorey seems to have been fascinated by the way he looked and what he wore, both of which remained remarkably consistent. Everyone commented on the beard and the jewelry, the fur coats and the sneakers. The curly beard changed from brown to grey to white, and the hair got sparser, but the clear blue eyes remained unchanged and so did the air, despite the jeans and the crewneck sweaters, of being part of another era. "Gorey appears to be a migrant from another century," Schiff wrote. "Beneath a baldish head and trifocals he wears a thick cloud of mustache and a white beard in the profuse, flowing style of a grand British litterateur." "Gorey's long fingers positively droop under the weight of the brass doughnuts he wears," said Mary Rourke in *The National Observer* in 1976. "They come from lands of mystery, like

Egypt and Tibet. And he wears dozens of African necklaces of beads and shells, jingling and clinking like odd bells. 'I've always dressed this way,' says Gorey."

In *City Poet*, his biography of Gorey's college roommate, the poet Frank O'Hara, Brad Gooch offered this description of the twenty-year-old "full blown eccentric" who arrived at Harvard in 1946: *Standing over six feet tall, thin and gaunt, Gorey accentuated the towering effect of his presence by dressing in long sheepskin-lined canvas coats and sneakers. Looking like a Victorian curiosity, Gorey invited inevitable characterizations from fellow students who perceived him as "tall and spooky*

*looking" or as a "specter." The costuming and gesturing, including, as one Eliot House neighbor recalls, "all the flapping around he did," decidedly cast him as a campus aesthete. "I remember the first day Ted Gorey came into the dining hall I thought he was the oddest person I'd ever seen," recalls the photographer George Montgomery, an Eliot House resident. "He seemed very, very tall, with his hair plastered down across the front like bangs, like a Roman emperor. He was wearing rings on his fingers."*

O'Hara and Gorey's close-knit circle during their Harvard years included the writer Alison Lurie and the poet V. R. (Bunny) Lang. Lurie provided a wonderful portrait of Gorey, only a few years out of Harvard, in a memoir of Lang. Gorey had recently moved to New York, but was back in Boston to visit his writer friends. "He came down in a faded pair of cotton pajamas, shrunk by the wash so that his long thin legs and long pale feet protruded in a comic-adolescent way," Lurie wrote. "As usual the top half of him did not match the bottom half. Over his pajamas he was wearing an Edwardian silk brocade dressing gown which he had picked up in a Third Avenue thrift shop, and, of course, his new curly brown beard, which had just about reached full growth."

Everyone was struck, too, by Gorey's distinctive voice and his even more distinctive way of speaking. "As Gorey talks, his voice soars and swoops enthusiastically across octaves, and his language takes on the high-flown rhetoric of a Victorian heroine or villain. . ." observed Dyer. "But he constantly brings his flights down to earth in the homey idioms of his Midwestern upbringing: 'Kiddo,' he calls himself; 'Heavens to Betsy!' he cries." Gorey's vaguely nineteenth-century presence and his meticulously wrought prose often seem to elicit a certain amount of high-flown rhetoric and deliberately obscure vocabulary from the people writing about him; describing Gorey's *The Fatal Lozenge*, Theroux called the dire alphabet book "an impious—but comic!—enchiridion of almost *all* violence." (The OED defines "enchiridion" as "a handbook or manual"). Anyone invited into any of Gorey's homes, whether the Murray Hill apartment where he lived during his thirty years in New York or either of the houses in Barnstable and Yarmouth Port on Cape Cod, itemized with amazement the yards of obviously often-read books and the miscellany of sometimes indescribable objects with which the writer and artist surrounded himself, not to mention the multiple, sometimes omnipresent, cats.

None of this—neither the playfulness, the charm, the sneakers, the cats, nor the erudition—comes as a surprise to anyone who has studied Gorey's unmistakable works attentively. As any alert Gorey-phile knows, his seemingly otherworldly little picture books are, in fact, full of complicated, sometimes contradictory allusions. Even the simplest Gorey image or the most straightforward line of prose frequently proves to reverberate with echos of its author's lifetime omnivorous reading and looking. Prodded by informed questions, Gorey was forthright about his sources, his working methods, and his influences. He would speak readily about the specific triggers for some of his books, and attempt to track the more intuitive, imprecise sources of others. Still, he usually avoided spelling out precise relationships. He spoke frequently of the French film pioneer Louis Feuillade as his primary influence yet he never explained just what the connections were. Perhaps he simply assumed that the origins of the iron railings and pompous furnishings of his settings or the prototypes for his characters' fantastic hats and handlebar mustaches or the models for their exaggerated gestures would immediately be obvious to anyone who had seen any of Feuillade's vivid shorts or haunting serials.

Nonetheless, such clues to the origins of Gorey's universe make us look freshly at his vaguely fin-de-siècle, vaguely British world of claustrophobic interiors and bleak landscapes. His allusions to Feuillade's weird synthesis of naturalism and fantasy make us think in new ways of Gorey's languid divas, his wide-eyed ingenues, his hearties in turtle-necks, and his sinister types in long padded dressing gowns. The bicycles, the motorcars, and the obsessively intricate wallpaper acquire new layers of associations. (By contrast, the cats and unnameable creatures, some small and agile, some domestic, and some monstrous, which vie for our attention with the urns and crumbling masonry, become wholly idiosyncratic.) Primed by Gorey's references to Feuillade, we begin to read his elliptical chronicles of the inexplicable as silent film intertitles raised to some transcendent level of literary excellence, compressed narratives told in meticulously honed sentences and elegant rhymes in which every word counts. In the same way, Gorey's casual acknowledgment that Buster Keaton was his favorite silent movie star makes us think differently about the air of deadpan reasonableness with which he recounts and depicts deaths and disappearances, the perfectly dreadful and the perfectly implausible.

However much or little they ultimately reveal, such glimpses into the workings of Gorey's always surprising intelligence not only provoke us into approaching his books in unexpected ways, but also reassure us that our half-formed associations with his images and texts are, as far as they go, accurate. Obviously, Gorey's work can be enjoyed without unraveling the complex skeins of reference (sometimes deliberate, sometimes not) that permeate his work. He himself seems to have been perplexed by innocent enthusiasm; he commented more than once on his amazement at being told that his brilliant parody *The Curious Sofa, a pornographic work* was the favorite book of some young child. But there is no doubt that even the most uncritical affection for Gorey's work is enhanced by realizing that there is more there than we imagined. The whole question of allusions, however, is made more complicated by Gorey's insistence that many seemingly overt references were probably

subliminal, the inevitable product of an imagination fuelled by decades of voracious reading and rereading, viewing and reviewing. Some appear to have surfaced almost without Gorey's consciously willing them, while others were deliberate homages. "The longer I go on," Gorey said in a 1998 interview with Christopher Lydon for National Public Radio, "the more I'm just grabbing at whatever happens to be around and hoping, you know, you can fit it in somewhere . . . some of it will be input from thirty years ago and some of it will be something I saw just yesterday."

Gorey wore his astounding erudition lightly. Self-deprecating, modest, always ready to laugh at his own foibles, he could happily skate on the surface of a conversation, in High Camp mode, and then suddenly reveal a hoard of staggering arcana. Sometimes he appeared to be gently teasing his interviewers, amusing himself without ever being condescending, and occasionally showing his hand. "Part of me is genuinely eccentric," Gorey declared to Lisa Solod of *Boston Magazine*, "part of me is a bit of a put-on. But I know what I'm doing." Predictable questions elicited predictable answers or, very rarely, exasperation. In response to some specially pedestrian inquiries about his apparent affinity to Edwardian England, Gorey wrote: "I suppose so to all of the above, more or less, he murmured reluctantly, but these are the sort of questions I think are worse than a waste of time to try and answer for reasons I have no intention of wasting more time in even adumbrating." But other questions, happily, provoked Gorey into unleashing idiosyncratic insights into literature, movies, dance, feline personalities, politics, sexuality, and much more. The person who emerges is not the familiar Gorey as a maker of cunning, and sometimes disturbing little books or of oddball theatrical entertainments, but as a ferociously intelligent, articulate, complicated, and perhaps ultimately unknowable individual with whom it is always surprising and enriching to spend time.

Contradictions abound. Gorey liked to present himself as frivolous, given to spending hours watching television reruns or avoiding doing any serious work. ("I'm a great one for drift," he said many times.) In fact, it quickly becomes evident that he was a disciplined, focused worker, an exacting writer and careful craftsman who not only completed and polished many more of the texts of his short "novels" than were published in his lifetime, but meticulously organized them, hoping to find time to illustrate them. Reading a series of interviews with Gorey can be rather like the way he himself described living with cats: "They have these mysterious lives that are only half-connected to you," he said. And on another occasion, still about cats: "It's very interesting sharing a house with a group of people who obviously see things, hear things, think things in a vastly different way."

The interviews in this collection have been arranged chronologically. They have been selected and edited to lessen repetitions—bearing in mind Gorey's observation that "the trouble with interviews is that you say the same things so often you end up believing them"—and not only to emphasize the breadth and depth of his interests and opinions, but also to allow readers to follow both the constancy and the alterations in his ideas, over time. Notes have been added to clarify some of the more obscure references and some less obscure ones not adequately identified in the text. Most of the interviews were clearly edited before publication. As Richard Dyer noted, "Gorey's mind is so fertile that his sentences begin and rebegin in a torrent of multiple possibilities. By the end, on the other hand, they tend to trail off inconclusively. Uncertainty and the fragility of every form of order are the subjects that underlie everything." None of the published interviews—of necessity—transmit precisely this quality of Gorey's conversation, nor do most of them replicate his unmistakable verbal delivery, described by Schiff as "the peaks and troughs of his inflections" or what Solod called his habit of "sprinkling his conversation with many 'you knows,' great, throaty laughs, and huge body sighs."

Gorey once said, perhaps facetiously, perhaps not: "I look like a real person, but underneath I am not real at all. It's just a fake persona." Perhaps not even Gorey's closest friends were privy to the full complexities of the independent-minded, thoughtful, and playful individual beneath the public façade, but the cumulative effect of the interviews he granted over more than twenty-five years is to offer a glimpse of that enchanting and sometimes exasperating person. A unique personality vividly emerges, like Gorey's work, full of contradictions and mysteries, but ultimately deeply absorbing, challenging, and entertaining, all at once.

—KAREN WILKIN

# Ascending Peculiarity

# And "G" Is for Gorey
# Who Here Tells His Story

Jan Hodenfield,

*New York Post*, 10 January 1973

Edward Gorey is sitting at a table at the Gotham Book Mart painstakingly painting the skirt of a dance costume depicted on the cover of his book *The Lavender Leotard*. He is applying watercolors to a quarter-inch square on the 1100 copies of the book because the printer couldn't manage the exact shade of the real skirt belonging to the New York City Ballet, of which Gorey is a devoted fan.

It's obviously a very important job to the 48-year-old master of the macabre and brahmin of the bizarre whose 30-odd books—very odd indeed—are the object of a rippling cult. Gorey himself is little known,

*A was an Author who went for a walk*

A was an Author who went for a walk

a man of his own shadows, and never gives interviews. He certainly didn't want to give this one. "On pain of death," he muttered when it was first broached. "Absolutely not," he said when asked directly. "I really haven't anything to say." But a gentle man and an eminently polite man, when tracked down at the Gotham, he diffidently gave in.

Face on he is the patrician as eccentric, with luxurious grey beard, melancholy crystalline blue eyes and the reluctant paunch of a frail man who's never had to worry about weight. His conversation is strewn with the land mines of anxiety—"if I don't kill myself to avoid coping with people," he says at one point, allowing at another that although his life often comes "to a screaming halt, I do manage to work." But his lack of interest in publicity, he says, is because "it doesn't really seem to be in aid of anything much. If it could make me rich as well as famous—but it doesn't."

Twenty years ago, when his first book was published, "I wanted to print it under a pseudonym—just an instinct actually. But I couldn't give a good reason. I think I was right at the time. I'm not someone easily unnoticed. I've always tended to run around in tennis shoes, fur coats, lots of jewelry. I just can't go out of the house with naked fingers."

It is suggested that the times have caught up with him and that the pressure must be off, but he sighs delicately.

"Well, nine years ago, if you were wearing nine rings when you went into a restaurant, people would not hesitate to ask you why . . ."

His first book was the result of a meeting with "the two gentlemen who ran Duell, Sloan and Pearce. They saw some drawings of mine. They suggested I do a book. Somehow or other I came up with *The Unstrung Harp*." That was an illustrated history of one Clavius Frederick Earbrass and, as in most of Gorey's work to follow, there was a sense of inexplicable, fey doom and a vividly imagined English Edwardian setting.

"No," says Gorey. "I've never been to England. I've never been out of the country. It all comes from reference books. I mostly read English literature. I've always liked Victorian novels. I don't like travel myself—who would take care of my three cats? They'd probably have a nervous breakdown—except they probably wouldn't even know I'd gone. I'm just a stick-in-the-mud type. I don't like upsets to my tummy, strange ringings in my ears, sleeping in strange beds."

Born and raised in Chicago, "I suppose I had a perfectly ordinary childhood, except that I was an only child. I did not grow up in a large Victorian house. I grew up in a series of apartments. My father was a newspaperman for the Hearst papers.

"I agree with people who say what happened after five is irrelevant but I don't remember what happened before then. I always did have a leaning to the bizarre, I guess. I was the kind of kid who thought it funny to throw an epileptic fit on the bus and that kind of thing. But I haven't the slightest idea why my work has taken the tack it has. I just do what occurs to me—if it occurs to me strong enough."

# The City Ballet
# Fan Extraordinaire

Anna Kisselgoff,
*The New York Times,* 13 November 1973

Nobody goes to the New York City Ballet quite as often as Edward
Gorey, who has attended virtually every performance here by the
company for the last seventeen years. After seventeen years of nightly
viewing, he can visualize the entire repertory, he says, "like a movie in
my head." "I can see everyone doing everything now," he adds. "I have
now reached the point where I can see Patty McBride[1] doing every ballet, even those she hasn't danced."

   Those who regularly spot Mr. Gorey in his fur coat, tennis shoes,
beard and grouse-hunter look at intermission sometimes make the mistake of assuming he is your all-purpose balletomane. Yet the Gorey

*Pas encore*

attraction is not to ballet in general but specifically to the City Ballet's repertory of ballets by George Balanchine.

"If you're absolutely obsessed with something, everything else seems meaningless," he admitted cheerfully. "I have really tried to appreciate other things." The classics leave him cold. "*Les Sylphides*? Where they're all looking for their contact lenses?" Sir Frederick Ashton's *The Dream*? "Sorry about that." *La Bayadière* in the Royal Ballet with its spectacular line of girls descending a ramp in arabesque? "Let's get just one of those girls come down the ramp as a token. I don't care how well organized they are."

What Mr. Gorey does care about is the Balanchine ballets and the changes in them that he has been particularly well equipped to observe throughout the years.

"Things do happen to ballets," he said in discussing *Agon*, considered the epitome of avant-garde ballet when Balanchine and Stravinsky created it in 1957. "At first you saw it and thought, what is everyone doing out there? You couldn't imagine what was going on."

"When you've seen a ballet as many times as I have, you get emotional about it. *Agon* was very different for the company that first did it. Everyone was screwed up to a pitch. Now they can do it like falling off a log. The formal qualities are a bit more obvious and everyone can't keep up with the original emotional pitch."

Mr. Gorey can remember when his favorite dancer, Patricia McBride, first stepped into the role of one of the bourgeois waltzing ladies in Balanchine's *Liebeslieder Walzer.*[2] She was, he said, "like a governess who had been invited because someone else didn't show up. Now she's the grandest."

One of the advantages of his marathon attendance at the City Ballet, Mr. Gorey explained, "is that you can see a person grow into a role."

"Of course there are performances I can barely sit through. But one of the things that made me go to every performance is that you may come across one that is going to be exceptional. I can count a great many transcendental performances that took place on a Saturday matinée when no one in his right mind would be there because they were doing *Firebird*, *Swan Lake*, and *Western Symphony*."[3]

Mr. Gorey began going to the City Ballet in 1953, three years after graduating from Harvard. By 1956, he was hooked. "I found myself going more and more often," he said. "There seemed no point in not seeing everything. It's easier to see every performance than to anguish which five performances out of eight to see.

"I do turn off in *Swan Lake*, it's true. I take little naps when the corps de ballet is thrashing through it and running about. Generally, I don't care what the casting for any ballet is going to be. I'm going to be there anyway. If it's going to be terrible, I'd rather not know in advance.

"After four or five weeks of repertory, you can get tired of going every day. I try not to do something strenuous during the day, especially during those five performance weekends. Virtually, my life is arranged around the New York City Ballet. I leave New York to work at Cape Cod the day after the season closes and I arrive back the day before it opens."

Balanchine is "the greatest living genius in the arts," Mr. Gorey declared. "Even if I don't like what he's done, I will sit around and fig-ure out what he's done because it's on such a high level. I hated his *Stars and Stripes*[4] at first and then I loved it. It's one of those ballets where the choreography is formally superb and no one realizes it because it's a fun ballet."

Mr. Gorey is frequently approached by total strangers for his views about this or that ballet performance. "Who needs opinions?" he said, thoughtfully.

I can hardly wait for the fall season, can you?

# Balletgorey

Tobi Tobias,

*Dance Magazine,* January 1974

As you should know, if you don't already, Edward Gorey is the tall bearded man in the voluminous fur coat and tennis shoes who appears on the first page of *The Lavender Leotard: or, Going a Lot to the New York City Ballet* to introduce "two small, distant, ageless, and wholly imaginary relatives" (more specifically, a girl child of about eleven and a boy of perhaps nine) to fifty seasons of the NYCB. In real life, and in similar garb, Gorey is, according to the friend who introduced us, "the only person who goes to every performance of the New York City Ballet. Even when they're doing *Nutcracker*."

Gorey's most salient characteristics, aside from the coat, the sneakers, and the specialized but quite formidable talent, are, in no particular order: searching intelligence, wit, introverted modesty, gentle kindness;

an affinity for the modes of Victori- and Edwardiana; a poignant sense of doom and loneliness; an unerring sense of style; a Harvard education with a concentration in French; a highly immediate feel for the vulnerabilities of childhood; a gradual, quiet success, with a growing following; a magnificently bushy grey beard and piercing clear-blue eyes; a penchant for wearing an extraordinary number of rings and keeping several cats.

Gorey works with a delicate, nervous line. In *Lavender Leotard* he creates pages of sensitive, helpless bodies with their own unballetic grace. These frail people have no physical clout whatsoever; they seem held together only by their extreme *raffinesse*. It's interesting to compare the delicacy and frailty of the *Lavender Leotard* figures to the finely etched but chunkily muscled dancers in *The Gilded Bat*, the author's only other venture into ballet-as-subject-matter.

The book is gently led through the company's aesthetic progress by three grave, well-dressed children. They appear sometimes as dancers, more often in impeccable street clothes of timeless classicity. Gorey recreates a world. Caricaturist not of personalities, but of events and ambiances, he chronicles the company's distinctive foibles, faults which have somehow become endearing to those of us who've seen the New York City Ballet through its lean years as well as the fat. There is its inability to cope with costumes and scenery, beginning with the poverty-stricken leotard and blue cyclorama days, when the company was rich only in aesthetic—"Don't you feel the whole idea of sets and costumes is vulgar?" Gorey recalls the endlessly unmatching pieces of the uncostumes, whence, the lavender leotard shown on the cover, with its accompanying skirt just a little too pink. Then we have the inevitable realization of the longed-for, corruptive money, when the ballerina floats in, beribboned and headdressed, in flower-decked tulle, to have her cavalier comment mildly, from amidst his flowing sleeves, "I didn't recognize you for a moment."

Deadpan, Gorey notes the chronic and incredible misuse of scenery: the Novice, dressed in her intestinal thing, with Nora's wet-locked hairdo, says to the G-stringed male bug she is about, somewhat reluctantly, to devour:[1] "Just once we could use the *Serenade* costumes and the backdrop from *Lilac Garden*."[2] Gorey crystallizes this tendency with a single picture and a few words: the children, as audience, tentatively leaning toward one another and whispering: "*Lilac Garden* again; those are the side pieces, and the bit across the middle must be the edge of *Swan Lake*."

Gorey takes us through the history and quirks of Balanchinean choreography: the strange movements and the difficult musicality—we have the pair from *Four Temperaments*[3] moving toward the wings like figures in an Egyptian frieze, body front, head and legs in profile, arms extended, flapping angularly down from the elbows, realizing, if they're in the same posture at the same time, "One of us is no longer with the music"; the characteristic pretzel convolutions; and the lesson Balanchine taught us over the years, dancers and viewers alike—to execute, see, and understand what we thought was impossible; delineating a configuration from the *Agon*[4] pas de deux—the girl in a vertical split along her partner's body—Gorey comments, "I can't imagine now why this ever seemed so difficult."

One of us is no longer with the music.

I can't imagine now why this ever seemed so difficult.

Of course, Gorey can't describe—only the actual experience could—just how beautiful and exciting those fifty seasons were. But he details everything around the beauty and excitement, which is enough to evoke it again for each of us, in the mind's eye, the gut, the secret heart, or wherever one's most vivid, passionate, lyric, and lavender images are stored. He recalls that long-gone yesteryear. And he sums up the snobbery we—surely America's most fanatical audience outside Ebbets Field—cultivated as ardent supporters of that odd and wonderful troupe: "Other companies merely put on ballets; we dance."

A small apartment building in Murray Hill,[5] incredible for its ornate iron work. "It's one flight up," Gorey calls, and immediately, for some inexplicable reason, I feel at ease. "I would apologize for the mess the place is in, but it's been this way for twenty years." His studio room is all books, lined with them, crazy stacks of them rising from the floor. A drawing board. A bed. Two ancient Noguchi lanterns. Two cats. *"I thought three."* "My Abyssinian is shy. She hides." Pictures revealing Gorey's interests—Victorian engravings, cats, some Orientalia, a few evil, enchanting monsters, a Francis Bacon postcard—and small, fascinating, rust-encrusted metal objects—scissors, old keys—cover the few unbooked vertical spaces. Dusty. Dim. Even the fireplace is stopped up with books. The kind of place in which only a fool would not feel comfortable. Home.

Gorey talks most easily about ballet, so that's what we talked about. Mostly. The new tape recorder, which neither of us knew very well how to work, was propped up on the overflowing drawing board, guarded by the larger, fiercely beautiful grey cat with the yellow eyes. I got the only chair—a drafting stool; Gorey, fidgeting with his many Indian silver rings, perched on the seat of a small stepladder; the black cat, vulture-like at first on the marble mantel, then, apparently concluding that we were up to no particularly unspeakable practices, dozing; stretching, elegantly lazy; dozing again.

This is the man who goes to every performance of the New York City Ballet.

**How did it begin?**

Well, I started going to ballet in 1937 or '38, in Chicago, when I was about twelve or thirteen. What first impelled me to go—no one in my family ever saw any ballet; oh, they might have gone to see Pavlova once, but they certainly weren't dance fans—was the decor. I was interested in art and I wanted to see the sets and costumes.

My first exposure to Balanchine's work was through Ballet Russe and Ballet Theater. I didn't like his stuff very much at the time, probably because it wasn't danced very well and then I just wasn't up to it yet. I was a real Ballet Theater nut, though; I adored *Scheherezade*.

I finished my (non-combatant) stint in the army in 1946, and went to Harvard. I didn't see Ballet Theater again until 1950, and by then, the first, fine careless raptures had worn off and I wasn't really terribly interested in them any more.

I came to New York to live in January 1953. I'd never seen the New York City Ballet before. I went to see them maybe three times that first winter. And the next year I went seven or eight times. And the year after that, a few more. And finally, by around '57 or '58, it had reached the point where it was just easier to buy tickets for every performance. By then I was absolutely hooked on Balanchine—to the point where, I'm afraid, everybody else bores me. Rather.

I feel absolutely and unequivocally that Balanchine is the great genius in the arts today. I've tried to figure it out, to myself, why what he does works so well. Whatever he does, no matter how often he changes it, or fiddles around with it, always the steps seem absolutely inevitable for the music at that given moment.

I'm not a great one for attending rehearsals, although I suppose, now, if I really wanted to, I could hang around the company twenty four hours a day. But occasionally, when George did *Requiem Canticles*, for example, I saw as many rehearsals as I could, because there was only going to be that one performance. I can't tell a thing from one performance of a Balanchine ballet. I usually dislike them the first time.

Balanchine is my life now. Just the fact of Balanchine's being here dictates so much of my existence. I'm sure I would have left New York years ago if it weren't for the New York City Ballet.

My nightmare is picking up the newspaper some day and finding out George has dropped down dead. Then, do I watch the company go into a slow decline or do I say "That's it. I saw it. It's past." and just go away?

I don't think the New York City Ballet is so far and away above every other company, the way Balanchine is so far and away above every other choreographer, but I think it's probably the best company I've ever seen. You can often hear me bitching about somebody's performance, but I'm bitching on a terribly high level.

**Is there a big difference between the character of the company now and the City Center days?**

It's hard to say. People are always asking me "What was it like in the old days?" I don't really know any more. A kind of legend's grown up about it, you know, that at City Center no one came except people who really loved ballet, and the house was always empty, but every one really appreciated it all. It's true, I think, that the subscription audience can be creepy; certainly the New York City Ballet's become more Establishment. And the Farrell[6] era certainly had its impact; for a while every girl in the corps was dancing like Suzanne. But when all is said and done, it's a pragmatic thing—this is what they're doing now, so why not enjoy it?

**What is your relationship to the company, exactly?**

Well, Eddie Bigelow,[7] the assistant manager, is a good friend of mine. I'm on casual terms with a lot of the dancers, not all of them, by any means. I'm occasionally invited to company parties. When I want to, like for the Stravinsky Festival, I was there for all the rehearsals, morning, noon, and night. But I didn't meet Lincoln Kirstein until about three years ago. And Balanchine, well, I've been at the same dinner party with him a couple of times. I find him difficult to talk to. What do you say to someone like Balanchine?

**Every performance? Really?**

I do go to every performance. You just don't know when somebody is going to turn up with a performance you're never going to forget. Those Saturday matinées when nobody is there and people are dancing like dreams.

When you do this, of course, you must realize that you're seeing something entirely different from everybody else. From someone who sees *Swan Lake* once a year. You become intimate with the work. With the way the dancers are performing. You begin noticing people in the corps. The choreography—I can still be brought up short by a ballet I've seen over a hundred times. I'll come out and say, "Was that little such and such always there in the third movement?" and they'll say, "Well, yes, it was," and I say, "Oh, I never noticed it before." Of course, your mind wanders a good deal.

**Do you go with particular people?**

I meet my friends.

**Do you care about the individual dancers? You must find some especially magical.**

Well, currently, Patty McBride is surely the greatest dancer in the world. Of course, my favorite dancer of all time is Diana Adams;[8] she was miraculous. She was crystal clear, absolutely without mannerisms, and she had one of the most beautiful bodies I ever saw in a ballet dancer—flawless proportions, those ravishing legs. Technically, well, she could make anything look effortless, like the Siren in *Prodigal Son*.[9] And the Second Movement of *Symphony in C*[10] is consecrated to her as far as I'm concerned—the way she could make it one long, seamless, legato line.

If I had to name the single greatest performance I ever saw, I'd say it was Diana rehearsing *Swan Lake*. She had no make-up on and a ratty old whatever dancers rehearse in, and she was chewing gum, and she walked through half of it, but it suddenly had all the qualities. . . . She was the kind of person who could extend herself on stage; her dancing made everyone else's look great.

And Kent[11]. This year in *Nutcracker*, she wasn't dancing all that well, but when she came to that final *penché* before the kids go drifting off again, I suddenly burst into tears because I thought, she *is* the Sugar Plum Fairy; she really is a figment of this little girl's imagination, and she's going to vanish into air when they leave; this whole thing will disappear like Prospero's island in *The Tempest*. She has this incredible kind of fragility, and an uncanny ability to make the choreography meaningful. But she doesn't always work the way she should, I'm afraid.

**What about Farrell?**

When she first joined the company I adored her and thought, she's so lovely, give her a chance. Well, they did. And then she developed that repertoire of mannerisms. Of course, technically, she could do anything, but she was often extraordinarily opaque about getting the meaning of the choreography across. It's too bad, though, that she's off in Béjart, doing her *penchés* into eternity. You know, I've always believed that the dancers who came off luckiest with Balanchine were the ones he was not totally obsessed with.

**And Kirkland?**[12]

A superb dancer who hasn't quite found herself yet.

**Tell me how anyone can sit through thirty-nine *Nutcrackers* in one season. Convince me.**

At first I thought, my God, this is the most boring ballet in the history of the world. Then I began to go more and more. People say, oh nothing much happens in the first act, but the second act is lovely. For me it's the first act that's so marvelous. It's an aspect of Balanchine's genius that nobody has paid much attention to. That party is one of the most enchanting things ever set on the stage. The relations between the children and the adults, everything—are breathtaking. It's a Platonic party, the essence of every family party—the way it should be and never is, the party that no one has ever attended. Every year it gets a little bit better.

Naturally, one of the reasons for going to *Nutcracker* is to watch the mice carry on—somebody's doing something crazy and new and different every night—and the tree grow, and the bed whiz around. And these days Shaun O'Brien, as Drosselmeir, gives a performance that holds the whole thing together; the instant he comes on you're riveted. The choreography for the Snowflakes is heaven. No one notices it because it's so pretty and they're busy watching the snow come down. And set back in time the way it is, it's nostalgic in a lost-world-that-never-really-existed way. Of course it's a very ambiguous ballet—frightening and funny and strange and beautiful—like most of George's work.

**Apart from the ballet, how do you spend the day? What about your own work?**

[He laughs, and begins to recite in how-I-spent-my-summer-vacation style.] I-usually-get-up-about-8:00. And if I can possibly find a reason for not setting to work, I do. On a good day I'll sit here and work for six to eight hours. The ballet at night. Or a movie.

I'm a real movie nut. Not that there's anything to see any more. I'm one of those people who feels the movies have been going downhill steadily since 1918. And that things really got bad when sound came in. But there were periods when I must have seen a thousand movies a year.

I used to go to the New York City Opera a great deal. But unfortunately they've gotten much more like the Met. I have bouts of concert-going now and then. But this last year I bought a new phonograph and I've been buying records like mad. I'll just sit here and play ten or twelve albums and that takes care of my concert-going, so to speak. I do some art galleries; that is, also, in spasms.

Of course the other half of my life is completely different, up on Cape Cod—Barnstable—where I have an aunt and a couple of cousins. I live in their house—I have the top floor, the attic—and I do all the cooking for the family, chauffeuring around, and so forth. I lead a very domestic existence up there.

**Getting back to the work, does it have a central importance for you?**

Well, if I'm not working on something of my own, I get very nervous and hung up. The rest of my life is a shambles, but I do try and continue to produce my own work. Because you get nagged by an idea until you do something.

**Have you had any formal art training?**

No. When I was in high school, I went to art school on Saturdays. That sort of thing. I've had very spasmodic and only rudimentary art training. Which I think shows only too clearly, but it's too late now to go and sit in life class from morning 'til night.

And then although I support myself by my art work, doing drawings for this and that, I tend to think of myself as a writer. My ideas tend to be first literary ones, rather than visual ones.

**What are your influences? There's a lot of very cerebral talk about the relationship of what you do to Lewis Carroll and Edward Lear.**

Well, Carroll and Lear are two of my favorite people. *Alice in Wonderland* is one of the earliest books I read and one of the books I know best. I'm an extravagant admirer of both of them and I'd love to be able to do things like they do, but I don't think I have. My influences have been elsewhere. The whole genre of nineteenth century book illustration—steel and wood engravings—holds a fascination for me. There's something in that technique that obviously appealed to me strongly. I'd pore over these books and of course everyone in them was in period costume. I do think period costume is more interesting to draw. My stuff is seldom very accurate Victorian or Edwardian of

*Pas ici*

course. And at times I have little deviations into the Twenties. I have, occasionally, drawn contemporary stuff, but I wouldn't do it in my own work, simply because my ideas don't lend themselves to contemporary life.

Then there's been a strong, direct influence from a certain kind of artist—[Paolo] Uccello, [Piero] della Francesca, [Georges] de la Tour, Vermeer, Balthus, Francis Bacon—who captures what you might call the frozen moment.

Literary influences? Well, the people I like—Jane Austen (my idol), Lady Murasaki—*The Tale of Genji*.[13] I'm very fond of Japanese and

Chinese literature. I like to work in that way, leaving things out, being very brief. Ronald Firbank.[14] Then later, [Samuel] Beckett, [Jorge Luis] Borges. I don't know if you'd call these influences. You simply feel affinities for other works of art.

**Often your work seems to be about children, or for children, or both.**

A lot of things I've done, I've intended for children. I don't know many children. And I don't know if I really remember what it was like being a child, or not. I use children a lot, because they're so vulnerable.

I am trying to reconcile this charming man's obvious achievement in his strange, brilliant work with the odd passivity of the dreamer-Gorey, who spends so much of his life watching Balanchine's dances and dancers, as if they recreate that beautiful lost world that never was. We're standing in the doorway, still talking, trying to keep the now-energetic black cat from escaping down the stairs and into the street. "One of the ballet mothers—who are a notorious breed, I must say—came up to me after she'd seen my show at the Gotham. She was very much taken with one of the drawings—she's a psychiatrist—and she said, 'I want you to tell me what that really means.' I would agree with George that when people are finding meanings in things—beware."

# Conversations with Writers:
# Edward Gorey

Robert Dahlin,
*Conversations with Writers*, Volume I, 1977

**H**ow did you get started doing art-word combinations?
I really don't know. I mean it all just sort of came. I started out writing plays.

**You did work on *Dracula*, didn't you?**
I designed *Dracula* for Nantucket three summers ago. They wanted to bring it to New York after Nantucket, but it turned out that the producer there had not gotten rights for anything but summer stock, because it hadn't occurred to anybody that there was a possibility of

Edward Gorey at
Francis W. Parker School,
Chicago, January 1940

anything else. And then an old fan of mine, Harry Rigby, you know, *No, No, Nanette* and everything. . . . Actually I met him maybe about a year before, and we were going to do something together, but it never panned out. Anyway, then he heard that I had done the *Dracula*, and without telling me he went out and got the rights for New York. The producers [in Nantucket] wanted to bring it in off-Broadway. And Harry was having delusions of grandeur. It happened that Josh Logan's wife had played the French maid in the original production back in 1927, so Josh Logan was presumably interested in directing it. Then

everybody's rights lapsed, I guess. Finally John Wulp, who had produced it on Nantucket, got the rights back for Broadway. So now I'm
redesigning the whole thing, and it's presumably coming into New
York on Halloween.

**Terrific timing.**

Yes. Well, it was supposed to go on this spring, but that didn't work
out, partly because I haven't finished the sets and costumes yet. Every
day or so they call up and scream, "Where is something more for something or other?"

**Does this *Dracula* stem back to when you were first beginning to write
plays?**

No, no, no. I'm just designing this. They're calling it my production,
which I think must make the director feel a trifle idiotic; it's the same
director as we had in Nantucket. Frank Langella is going to play
Dracula, supposedly. The producer, John Wulp, is very nice, and he is
shielding me as much as possible from all this nonsense. It's the first
time I've ever designed a Broadway show, certainly.

**When did you begin writing plays?**

I started writing plays when I was in the Army for no very good
reason that I can recollect now. I've always drawn. I never knew what I
wanted to do when I was a child. After I was in the Army I ended up at
Harvard in a sort of inadvertent way. I was drawing and writing,
taking creative writing courses: you know, the whole bit.

**Were you trained as an artist?**

Not really very much. I used to take Saturday classes at the
Art Institute in Chicago from time to time. I actually went to the Art

Institute for one term after I got out of high school, then I switched over to the University of Chicago. But I was promptly drafted—so much for that. My first publisher saw some of my drawings and stuff and got interested. I didn't have anything that would make a book at the time.

**Who was your first publisher?**

It was Duell, Sloan & Pearce, which is no longer in existence. My first two books were with them. They didn't make any money, nor did you get paid much attention. Great piles of those books were remaindered on 42nd Street for nineteen cents several years later.

**What were those?**

*The Unstrung Harp* and *The Listing Attic*. God, I wish I had those copies now. I remember that I bought fifty of each when they were remaindered for nineteen cents, and I don't know what happened to them. I wouldn't have thought I knew fifty people, much less fifty people I was planning to give away a book to. I have one battered copy of everything I've done at this point. I've got an apartment that consists of nothing but books; on the other hand, I don't collect. It's a mania to buy books. I can't go out without buying a book. But it would never occur to me to collect. I collect authors because obviously I want all their work, but this business of first editions and that whole thing doesn't strike me.

**How did *The Unstrung Harp* and *The Listing Attic* come about?**

Well, *The Listing Attic* was the limericks I had been writing for years, but I never had done any drawings for them.

**Did you plan to publish them?**

No—I don't know. I don't know what I thought I was doing. I mean why was I writing plays that obviously couldn't be put on? They were like ten pages long and demanded the technical powers of the Metropolitan Opera stage to get put on, what with the special effects and everything. I remember I started writing *The Unstrung Harp* to order, except I don't know if anybody gave me the idea for it. They just said give us an idea for a book that you think we might find feasible. Why they found that feasible, I cannot imagine at this late date. Just about that time I moved to New York, after I had been living in Boston for two and a half years. After I got out of Harvard I came down to visit New York and was offered a job at Doubleday and turned it down at first, because I didn't want to live here. I wasn't starving to death. I started out as an artist in the art department, then I switched over to being a book designer. I was there seven years in all.

**How did you come to the attention of Duell, Sloan & Pearce?**

I had an English teacher at Harvard, John Ciardi,[1] the poet, and I got to know him fairly well. He knew Merrill Moore,[2] the psychiatrist and poet. I think Merrill somehow introduced me to Mr. Pearce and Mr. Duell in Boston. They saw some of my drawings and were interested, Mr. Pearce especially. As I say, they asked me to try and think up an idea for a book. And I guess I did, because they published [*The Unstrung Harp*] in the fall of '53—which meant that I came to New York in January of '53. So I must have done the book before I came here. Then *The Listing Attic*, which was the limericks—I had enough for a book. And then I didn't have anything published for nearly three years, when Doubleday published two books of mine, which is only the beginning of a lurch from one publisher to another.

From Number Nine, Penwiper Mews,
There is really abominable news:
    They've discovered a head
    In the box for the bread,
But nobody seems to know whose.

**Your books are, I think, an acquired taste. You have to get to know them to understand the way you work. Is that why you changed publishers?**

No. I never changed publishers; they always changed me, as it were. They all thought they were going to make more of a splash with whichever particular book they were doing at the time. And then they'd do like one or two, and the splash didn't arrive. So they would say reluctantly, "Well—"

**One of your books was published by the Fantod Press.**

Oh, that's me. I published, let's see, I guess fourteen of my own and will continue to do so at intervals. I've been doing it for a long time, because there were periods when I had all sorts of things that hadn't been published. Finally I ran out of stuff.

**What does it feel like to be a cult figure, which I think you certainly are?**

I'm afraid so. I'm not sure. See, I've been going to the New York City Ballet ever since I came to New York, virtually every performance. So there are endless numbers of people who don't know who I am, but know me from the New York City Ballet. So if I'm caught someplace else, voices will come out of the dark saying, "What are you doing here?" And I think, "What do you mean what am I doing here?" Sometimes they won't even explain. Then they'll usually say, "Why aren't you at the New York City Ballet tonight?" or something. And when the New York City Ballet was on strike, people used to come up and commiserate with me in the streets and say, "Oh, you poor boy! What are you planning to do?" Also, there's no use denying that my physical persona is about as eccentric as you can get.

**Oh, well, I think you've got some way to go before you get that eccentric.**

I mean, for instance, I walk a lot, and I'm always walking in the same places and everything. So people who do not know me just recognize me. But then, of course, there are the people who do know who I am. It's always flattering to have someone come up and say, "I love your work." But, on the other hand, what do you say after "Thank you" and that sweet smile I put on? After all, I've been doing this for twenty-five years almost. So now it's: "Oh, you've been one of my childhood idols for as long as I can remember." You know what I think? "Am I really that much older than you are, whoever you happen to be?" I've decided that, as somebody's pointed out, the older you get, it's very difficult to tell how much younger anyone else is. I mean I can't really tell the difference now between people who are fifteen and people who are thirty-five. When that first started happening, it did rather flabbergast me.

**Do you start out with a notion of what you are going to do, or for the whole of a book?**

No, not really. I think you have to sit around waiting for the initial idea. I don't think you could just sit down and say, "I'm going to write a book about such and such." You've got to get the idea from somewhere, wherever it seems to come from outside. It always seems to me that there has to be some little seed or something.

**What would have been the seed for *The Hapless Child* or *The Curious Sofa*?**

*The Hapless Child*—I happen to know what that comes from. It was a French movie dating, I think, about 1905 or 1906, called *L'Enfant de Paris*. I can't remember the director.[3] I only saw it once. At one point the Museum of Modern Art started to go through its entire film collection on Saturday mornings. You could subscribe to it. For years, we'd just sit upstairs on Saturday mornings, and we'd watch all these movies that hardly ever get shown otherwise. I know that the movie starts out exactly the way *The Hapless Child* does. *The Hapless Child* deviates quite early. But I've always been a passionate moviegoer. I've been very much influenced by old movies, and a lot of my books derive, in one way or another, from old movies. That one, I remember, quite impressed me; I can remember sitting in the dark and thinking, "Oh, what a zippy movie." Actually it was, I think, the little girl in the movie who was kidnapped and taken down to the Riviera and was finally ransomed in the end. The plot was entirely different.

I think maybe the business about the father returning was from the movie. But it had a totally happy ending. As I say, it was just the opening part of it which somehow set me off, and I remember jotting down a couple of salient points in the dark. *The Hapless Child* is the one book, I remember, in which I was on about drawing number five, drawing wallpaper, and I thought, "I'm so bloody bored drawing wallpaper. I can't stand this." So I put the book aside for about five years. Then suddenly I felt, "Well, I better finish this up." So I went back to drawing wallpaper and finished the book.

**I must say that's the one thing that's true about your art: there are a lot of lines there.**

Yeah, but a lot of people draw a lot more lines than I do. Somehow I think I manage to give the effect of having drawn more lines than I have or something. I'm not really all that intricate. I mean I'm intricate, but there are other people, I think, who spend a lot more time at their drawings than I do.

**How long does it take you to do a drawing? Every one must be different.**

The complicated ones are somewhere between a whole day and part of the next maybe—one or two days. I work reasonably rapidly when I'm working, which is sometimes very little.

**Do you develop it as it goes along, or do you have it pretty well mapped out by the time you sit down?**

The one thing I did learn very early was that I had to have the text completely written before I could do the drawings. I mean I can start by doing the drawings, it wasn't that. It was if I started the drawings, I'd never finish the text. I had to know how it was all going to come out before I could. . . . That is one of my problems now: I mean I have something like fifty or sixty texts waiting for illustrations. Then I have God knows how many more that are partially written. I will probably finish those since I have . . . Well, I can still remember things that I didn't finish as a child and feeling so guilty about it. So I haven't for twenty-odd years, I don't think, started something I didn't eventually finish.

**As you're writing a text you must have an idea of what you're going to use for illustrations.**

No, I trust myself enough so that I don't have to say to myself: "Will this make a drawing?" I think my subconscious takes care of that. When I'm writing occasionally I'll have a momentary block, or I'll think "What made me think I could do a drawing for this particular sentence?" but I can usually solve it. I can quite often begin by doing a drawing of something completely different so that it will make a counterpoint.

**You said you work pretty quickly. Are you disciplined?**

No, I will do practically anything rather than sit down and work. With the slightest reason to go out of the house, the day is shot. Success really does nothing for one, I've decided, at all. I used to think, "Oh, God, if I only didn't have to illustrate these dreadful books for other people"; not necessarily that they were dreadful books, but they weren't my own. Sometimes I quite liked the book, but I thought, "I can't illustrate that," and ended up doing a terrible job. In other books that weren't really very good and that I didn't particularly like, I ended up doing a fairly good job, or at least I thought I had. It didn't make any difference whether I liked it or disliked it, or how I felt at the time, or anything else. But just think—how marvelous to work only on my own projects. Well, now basically that's all I do. And yet it's worse somehow. I must say *Dracula* is not a project I would have ever taken to my bosom if they hadn't offered lots of money. Not that I have anything against it; it just doesn't interest me very much. I keep telling everybody plainly that what I really want to do is design sets and costumes for Gilbert and Sullivan or something like that. So far no one has taken me up on that. I have done a couple of ballet sets and I am also doing a Dracula book, which I am not really sure I want to do.

**A book based on the play?**

It's all sort of lunatic. I haven't started on it yet because I have to get the sets and costumes done. What it's basically, in theory, going to be is a kind of synopsis of the play in my own manner, but I suspect it's going to get further and further away so it will not bear any relation to anything. Presumably the backgrounds of the drawings will look like the stage and the costumes will be the costumes of the play. I'm certainly not going to try and reproduce the people, especially since nobody knows who will be in it anyway.

**You are a noted macabre, of sorts.**

Which I don't really believe in either so much. It sort of annoys me to be stuck with that. I don't think that's what I do exactly. I know I do it, but what I'm really doing is something else entirely. It just looks like I'm doing that.

**What are you doing?**

I don't know what it is I'm doing; but it's not that, despite all the evidence to the contrary.

**Do you see yourself as a teller of moralistic fables?**

I don't know what anybody else's point of view really is, of course, Actually, the content always sort of takes care of itself because I don't think one has any control over that anyway. Usually what sets me off is the kind of formal aspect of it. I can't think of a good example of exactly what it would be like. I can think better in terms of ballet: it's like doing a ballet with only a certain kind of steps. Obviously nobody ever says "I'm going to do a ballet in which nobody does such and such." There's a section in a Balanchine ballet where the girl is manipulated by four men and never touches the ground.[4] I'm sure that when he started out to do it he didn't say, "Well, I'm going to do a piece where the girl never touches the ground." But obviously, since he works very fast anyway, he probably got it all done and suddenly realized that she hadn't touched the ground. Sometimes I will take about equally from life, or from other artwork, or another book. I'm very, very catholic in my choices—sometimes it's dance; sometimes it's movies; sometimes it's other books; sometimes it's pictures. It may be verbal; it may be visual.

**Inspirations?**

Yeah, I tend to be very imitative, so if I see something I like, I think, "Oh, I'd love to do something like that." Well, no matter how hard you try to do that, of course, eventually you wander off on something completely different. The original impetus may be totally goofy. I remember, and I really still don't know what the connection is, *The Wuggly Ump* started from a book about that size. I don't know what the text said because it was in German; it was by Christian Morgenstern.[5] But it was a little Easter book with rabbits and eggs and God knows what else. What that has to do with *The Wuggly Ump*, do not ask me. I think about the only thing that is left is that the books are the same size; the pictures are the same size.

***The Wuggly Ump* is sort of unusual. Most of your books aren't in color, are they?**

No. I can work in color, but I don't often. Partly the reason I've never worked in color to begin with is that since I was working at Doubleday I knew only too well that if nobody knew who you were or anything, they weren't going to publish books in color. A lot of my books were intended as children's books, and they would not publish them as such, which I always thought was very shortsighted. [*The Wuggly Ump*] is the only one that's ever been published as a children's book.

**So your inspiration comes from any number of things and this will be the kickoff for a whole book?**

Yeah. Unfortunately, as the years have gone by, I can now practically conceive a book in about three minutes, which is all I need. I used to worry endlessly about what if I dry up? What if I never have another idea? While I would not like the feeling of never having another idea again, I can certainly do without very many more, because obviously I'm never going to finish the ones I've got.

**You've got a long time to go yet.**

Well, one hopes. I still have this whole backlog of stuff which I feel sitting up there waiting to fall on me if I don't get it done.

**You must plot easily, I guess. I mean if you can call . . .**

Yeah—if you can call it . . . I'm a firm believer in plotting. I know that sounds sort of silly, but I'm a firm believer in the plot as the underpinning of everything else. If you don't have a plot, you're in trouble. Or at least if you don't have a plot you ought to have something else in mind to substitute for it.

**Do you revise as you go along?**

Yeah, I have to get the first sentence right or I can't do the second, and so forth. I can cover several hundred pages with versions of the first sentence. Actually I write easier than I used to. I mean I used to agonize. I also discovered that sometimes the revision just gets you nowhere; you might as well go back to what you've done in the first place. Occasionally I will get stuck.

**You're more of a cat person than a dog person, but you have more dogs than cats in your books.**

I left cats out for a long, long time. I don't know, maybe I was superstitious about putting them in or something. Even now I don't. My anthropomorphic cats are really something quite different from regular cats.

**Do you find it easy to create characters—for instance, the people from *The Loathsome Couple*?**

I suppose it was obvious that [*The Loathsome Couple*] was based on the Moors Murders, which disturbed me very greatly for some reason. I'm a great aficionado—that's the word everybody uses —of true crime.

**Wasn't there a woman who wrote about it?**

Oh, Pamela Hansford-Johnson[6] wrote that sort of dodge, which I sort of agree with, as I remember, about one of the reasons the murders were committed was because of all the nasty things the murderers had been reading.

**Pornography, right?**

Well, in a way, that book is a kind of equivalent to *The Curious Sofa,* because I had read very little pornography in my life. And if you will notice it, *The Curious Sofa* begins the same way as *The Story of O,*[7] which is what finally set me off—where I think he picks her up in the park and puts her in a taxi after that. But I once remember spending an absolutely paralyzingly wet Sunday afternoon in Chicago reading *The Hundred and Twenty Days of Sodom* by the Marquis de Sade in French. I got so bored; I was ready to blow my brains out after wading through that. But I always wonder how people can manage to write pornography. The first couple of pages are fun, but after that I just get . . . There are only so many things that you can do and so forth and so on. And so *The Curious Sofa* I wrote over a weekend and did the drawings.

**Over a weekend?**

Yeah. I just sat down and wrote it as fast as anything I've ever written, and I did the drawings just about as quickly. You know, there were two printers that turned it down.

**Not because it was pornographic?**

Well, no. One of them said they simply wouldn't do it. The other said that if we would remove the word "pornographic" from the cover they would print it. I think, in a way, *The Curious Sofa* is possibly the cleverest book I ever did. I look at it, and I think, "I don't know quite how I managed this because it really is quite brilliant." I don't like it, but you know, I'm really quite fond of its cleverness—the fact that everybody's names are totally indistinguishable. People used to approach me to illustrate pornographic novels after that. And I would say, "Have you looked at the book?" The men are totally indistinguishable from the women; everybody is seen from behind. That's the whole point: I think it's really about a girl who's got an obsession for grapes more than anything else.

But *The Loathsome Couple* was the same sort of thing. I resisted writing it for quite some time, and it really is one of those things I had to get off my chest. I sat around with a manuscript for a long, long time. *The Soho Weekly News* was always saying they would print anything. I thought, "All right, print this." And so I did it and I purposely made the drawings as red and a certain gray and dull and, you know, sort of unpleasant, uncharming as I could and everything. I was looking at it again, and it really is even more unpleasant than I thought.

**I don't have a great affinity for children, so that may be why I enjoy the book.**

Well, after all, I've been murdering children in books for years. It's much more personal to me in a way, I suppose, than a lot of the others, because I really read those books about the Moors Murders. Somehow it stuck in my mind: This is really one of the great unpleasantnesses of all time.

**So *The Loathsome Couple* is more of a sociological comment?**

I guess. I don't know what it is. I was looking at it, and I thought, you know, "What is all this in aid of, exactly?" I remember thinking of some of the little jokes, or what seemed like jokes to me; like the meal—I spent a long time figuring out what they should have to eat.

**Artificial grape soda was first.**

There were lots of versions of that until I got it right down to my likings. And I saw in them a lot of myself, like the comment, "Even as a child she had thick ankles and thick hair." I kept thinking, "Had I better remove that sentence?" I couldn't quite. I finally decided to leave it in, but I'm not sure about it even now. I know one is always supposed to throw away one's best lines.

**What do you mean?**

Well, you know, if you've got something really spiffy you should throw that out because the rest is obviously not up to it. Quite often I have discovered this to be true. Since my things aren't all that long, quite often I throw away the first sentence and start with the second, as it were.

**Are there things that you would change now if you were to go back and redo?**

I doubt it. I always feel that whatever you did at the time was obviously what you had in mind. I hardly ever reread any of my stuff anyway, in any real sense of the word. I used to worry about repeating myself, but I thought, "Well, I can't sit down and read my collected works every time before I start anything, or else I'll go crazy." So now I just hope that it's something slightly different from anything I've done before.

*and the tea-urn empty*

**Do you have a favorite book?**

I tend to like the ones that make the least obvious sense. I'm very fond of *The Nursery Frieze*. And I'm very fond of *The Untitled Book*, or at least I think I am; as I said, I don't look at them. I've always rather liked *The Object-Lesson*, because that doesn't make any sense. Those kinds of things are harder to do than almost anything else, so I feel I've done them reasonably well. I haven't done anything of my own that I didn't believe in. And I don't think the amount of work you have to put into anything has got anything to do with it. As I say, *The Curious Sofa* took me less time than anything else I've ever done. I do tend to sort of write the things that would make as little sense as possible. I have always been sort of fascinated by that; you know, Flaubert's idea of writing a novel about nothing. Most minimal art drives me absolutely crazy. In fact, most of what I do would drive me crazy in anybody else. I can find myself getting very upset by somebody else doing the same thing, I think.

**Is there something that has influenced you, like writing a novel about nothing?**

Well, that's one of those tag lines that has always stuck in my head. It's more an example. *The Object-Lesson*, for instance, really grew out of Samuel Foote's poem called *Grand Panjandrum*.[8] It's a short eighteenth-century poem. He was a playwright, but he tossed off these ten or twelve lines. I cannot really repeat them to you, but it's a complete nonsense poem. The thing was that somebody said they could memorize anything if they heard it once, so he tossed off this total nonsense. I don't know if the person managed to repeat it or not, but anyway it turns up in anthologies of nonsense verse and children's verse. It makes no sense at all. Randolph Caldecott[9] has done illustrations for it which are quite wonderful. Anyway, as I say, I purposely sat down with the object to write a piece that made no sense. That took me a long time to do. There were endless versions to that I had floating around somewhere.

**Is there any humorist or commentator or artist who has influenced the way you have developed?**

I think actually the biggest influences on me have been things that are totally indirect. I mean I've been going to the New York City Ballet for just under a quarter of a century now, almost every performance. And George Balanchine's choreography has had—it's totally impossible to put into words—but somehow the way he works has influenced me a great deal. The way he works with the dancers; in a sense I'm trying to emulate his thinking. From the authors that I admire most I'm totally different; I mean Jane Austen is absolutely my favorite author in the whole world, closely followed by Lady Murasaki and Anthony Trollope. I'm a great admirer of great, long nineteenth-century English novels. Nineteenth-century engraving, of course, has had an enormous influence on me. My work doesn't really look like that, but it obviously derives from that.

**In this combination of pictures and words, how do you see yourself—as an artist, or as a writer, or as an amalgam of the two?**

Well, I suppose, really, it's a combination of the two. In a sense I think of myself as a writer more, but that isn't true either. It's not that I'm just illustrating my own work.

**So you would want to be remembered as a writer of interesting little books?**

Well, yes, I suppose. Until about, let's see, it would be about three years ago, I guess, I hadn't done any drawing that wasn't for a book for over twenty years, probably. I hang on to the drawings for my books anyway because we were hoping that Mr. Andreas Brown at the Gotham Book Mart could sell my archives and I could retire or something or other. In any case, I probably have all the drawings for my books. And so when the question of having a show at the Graham Gallery[10] came up, I had to do all new stuff. That was the first time I had done any drawing just for the sake of drawing for a long time and it was fun to do. But even then my mind tends to work in such a way— well, like the last show that I had, I did this one drawing just sort of off the top of my head and suddenly a whole book came to me, which eventually I will do. I just tend to think in series of things that will turn into books.

**Despite your love of ballet, I think you've done only one book about it.**

Well, there's *The Gilded Bat*, and then I've done a thing for the New York City Ballet called *The Lavender Leotard*. I do things like postcards and posters and buttons for the New York City Ballet Guild. I'd like to do a ballet alphabet book. I like alphabet books, you know; they're already ready-made, shaped, too. I've got a few alphabet books I've never gotten to.

**What are you trying to do in an alphabet book?**

*The Fatal Lozenge* is the first one.

**This would certainly, I would think, characterize you as someone with a bit of a macabre . . .**

Well, yes. This was a very early book and at that date I was not above trying to shock everyone a bit.

**Do you have an idea who your audience is?**

Well, I can only go by the people who come up to me. There are obviously a lot of college people and even some high-school ones, I think. And I suppose they are more "sophisticated," whatever that may mean.

**I would think some of the books would be too sophisticated for a high-school group.**

Well, people who have been reading my books for a long time often say they've seen their children around the house with them. I obviously have a certain following with small children. Someone I know said quite seriously that *The Curious Sofa* was their child's favorite book. I don't know what the child thought was going on. Of course, I was a very precocious reader as a child. I learned to read by myself when I was about three and a half or something. I can remember reading *Dracula* when I was about seven, and it scared me to death, but I can't imagine what I was getting out of it. A lot of it must have been totally over my head. I remember reading all the novels of Victor Hugo when I was about eight, which is more than I can do now. I started trying to read one a couple of years ago. Tedium, dear God. I still remember Victor Hugo being forcefully removed from my tiny hands when I was about eight, so I could eat my supper. They couldn't get me to put him down.

**I'd hate to have to explain *The Curious Sofa* to a child.**

Well, I would too, but I don't know. . . .Well, any of the other ones for that matter.

**How did you get involved in doing the invitation for the book party for Allegra Kent? Was that just out of friendship?**

Yes. I know a lot of ballet dancers, but I did not know Allegra Kent. She's always been one of my favorites but I'd never met her. One day my phone rang and this chirpy little voice came over the phone, "Hello, is this Edward Gorey?" I said, "Yes." She said, "This is Allegra Kent." And I thought, "Oh, sure, honey. Now tell me something new." Anyway it was very ambiguous what she said. She said, "I've done this book on water exercises[11] and I want to send it to you." I thought she was sending me manuscripts because she wanted me to illustrate them or whatever. So I was sort of startled by this, because I always worshipped at her shrine. Then I thought, "This is the kind of joke that people usually pull on people." I was talking to somebody a day or so later and I said, "Oh, listen. I had the goofiest phone call a couple of days ago." I told them about it. They said, "Oh, that was Allegra. That's very Allegra." Indeed, about a week later the book arrived. Then she started sending me notes and things. She does things like write a note and then stitch it up inside a paper bag and mail it. I was just crazed, but it was very amusing. And then I got a letter from Washington, and she said, "Would you, could you possibly do a drawing for the invitation for a party being given for the book?" and I said, "Oh sure, I'd love to." So finally I met her. Funny—I ran into her on the street one day and said, "Oh, listen, Allegra, I think it's time we met."

The party was very strange, There were very few people from the ballet there, like five people. I had gotten invited on the strength of having done the invitations and stuff. Anyway, everybody was standing around, and I said in one of my best loud flippant voices, "Who are all these people, do you suppose?" There was this middle-aged lady, whose husband came up and said, "Oh, well, listen, we're old friends of Allegra's." I made it worse; I said, "Well, I didn't mean *you*." But everybody looked very odd.

**Ms. Kent's book is about exercise in water.**

Yeah. You put on these little, tiny water wings, which you clamp on to your wrists and your ankles, and you overcome gravity. She gave us a demonstration in the pool. The pool was filled with camellias stapled to water-lily petals. Oh dear.

**How many languages do you speak?**

I don't speak any. I majored in French at Harvard but my French is absolutely atrocious.

**Some of your limericks are in French.**

But they are very inaccurate. Edmund Wilson castigated me wildly for them. He was always castigating me for my prose. That's why when I finally dedicated a book to him, it had no text. I thought, "That will fix you, Edmund. Now what will you be able to say?"

**Did he castigate you in a review?**

No, no, no. The poor man did that one piece on me in *The New Yorker*[12] once after I had only four books published, and everybody's been quoting from it ever since. He was a very sweet man. He intimidated me terrifically. I finally first met him at a New Year's Eve party when we both got wedged behind the same sofa. I don't hear very well in noisy places, so I couldn't hear most of what he was saying. He was very formidable anyway, though very nice. And the last time I saw him at the Princeton Club, deafness had ensued for all of us. I was trying to figure out what he was saying and he was trying to figure out what I was saying; both of us were trying to figure out what the third person present was saying. This was not too long before he died.

**Have you written any books that are all text?**

The Black Doll.[13] I was hoping to make it into a movie sometime. It was very seriously intended as a movie. I tend to drift my way through existence, and if I had decided to direct myself a little more than I ever did, I think I probably would have worked in the theater more. I was connected with this thing called the Poets' Theater[14] of Cambridge while I was at Harvard and afterwards. I loved it. It was kind of a goofy amateur theater where we all did the very arty plays and so forth. It was great fun, but when I came to New York I didn't particularly care for the equivalent of it. Nobody has ever asked me to do anything particular, so . . .

**Why did you publish some books under a pseudonym?**

I wanted to publish everything under a pseudonym from the very beginning, but everybody said, "What for?" And I couldn't really explain why I wanted to. I still don't know exactly, except that I think what you publish and who you are are two different things. I don't really see that much connection.

# The Dick Cavett Show with Edward Gorey

Dick Cavett,

*WNET*, New York, November 30, 1977

Good evening. Every artist creates his own world, and tonight I want to welcome you to the particularly mysterious, macabre world of Edward Gorey. If you're not an addict of his work, you might not know what to expect when you first see it. Of course, you wouldn't. You never forget Gorey's work once you have been exposed to it, and you will certainly never come across anything like it elsewhere. Although I want to ask him a question about that. I would like to introduce you to the author and the artist himself Edward Gorey. How do you do, sir?

How do you do?

The author introduces two small, distant, ageless, and wholly imaginary relatives to fifty seasons of the New York City Ballet.

Years ago, someone with wonderful taste and precognition gave me a copy of *The Listing Attic*, and I thought, "I must be the only person in the world who's ever heard of, or seen, this mysterious, wonderful sort of work."

You probably were, at the time.

**Well, this would have been about 1956, '58—*The Listing Attic*?**

Yeah. Yeah, it came out in 1954.

And then I began to find that there were other Gorey cultists. And rumors that you didn't exist; that you lived in an abandoned submarine; that you wore a cape everywhere; that you were only out at night; you know, that you molested the library books that you checked out. You know, just the strangest . . . because you must know the kind of rumors that have circled about your name and myth. Have you ever been on TV?

No.

He explained himself Unconvincingly.

**Are you enjoying it so far?**

Painless so far.

**Do you want to see what you look like on television?**

No. No, I don't.

**If you look over there you will.**

Yes, I realize.

**If you'd rather not —-**

I'd rather not.

**OK. Seeing your drawings, I had a sense of déjà vu. I had a feeling that I had seen Henry James illustrated by you. Is that just that one gets a feeling from Henry James that is Gorey-like?**

I suppose. When I first came to New York, I worked for Doubleday and, among other things, I did covers for Anchor Books paperbacks. And I did several Henry James, which were highly thought of.

**Aha.**

And I've always had this very ambivalent feeling towards Henry James. I think I've read practically everything he's ever written, and I loathe and detest all of it.

**I have the same mixed feelings about him. Someone said that following through one of his sentences is like watching an elephant try to pick up a pea.**

Well, that's true. You know, there are certain things of James I think are—some of the short things. Well, *The Turn of the Screw* and *The Aspern Papers*.

***The Turn of the Screw* is made for you, isn't it? It has several things that are characteristic of your work. The children . . .**

No. Something like that I think is—I mean, it could be illustrated—but it's superfluous to illustrate. People are always coming to me to illustrate things that really do not need to be illustrated. I mean, that I really think would be better off not illustrated, because I think the illustrating of horror stories is one of the nightmares of my existence. Because people still ask me to do it a lot. And, for one thing, in illustrating a horror story, you obviously cannot illustrate what's horrible.

**No.**

I once did a whole anthology of horror stories and by the time I was through, I was practically faint on the floor, because I couldn't—I was trying too hard to avoid, you know, giving anything away. So that you could usually only illustrate the first couple of pages before the story got going.

**That's right. If you do *The Tell-Tale Heart* and show the man under the floor—**

There's no use reading the story.

**Now we've spoiled it for a number of people.**

Right. Yes.

**One of the things that recurs in your work is the beset-upon child, the murdered child, the abused child. I was going to ask you the obvious question, of what you were like as a child. I'm sure amateur psychiatrists have said, "Well, he obviously had a wretched, horrible, baroque, macabre childhood."**

No, I didn't. I had a typical sort of Middle-Western childhood in Chicago, in the suburbs.

**You're not putting me on.**

No, no.

**You have been known to put an interviewer on.**

Not really, I don't think. But I was an only child. Apart from that . . .

**You didn't lurk in dark alleys, or . . .**

No, no. You know, I would like to think that I was much more poetic and sensitive than anybody else, but I don't think it was true.

**And you didn't have an unusual—**

Now I wish I had kept my collection of comic books.

**So do I—yes. I had all the original Captain Marvels, I think. But you were not lured into garages by strange people?**

No.

**Any more than the average child? Any more than I was?**

I think less.

**Oh, really?**

I don't remember ever being lured anywhere by anybody.

**Oh, yes. I was lured into a number of garages—but we'll go into that some other time. You WERE a child, of course, and someone once asked you what you were like as a child, and you said "small." You favor the monosyllabic response to some of the more obvious questions?**

Well, I start to babble very easily, so it's sometimes better.

**Do you like children?**

I don't really know any. I have one small first cousin, once removed, who will be eleven this year, and that's about the only child I know to any extent.

**So you might like them if you happened to run across one.**

Oh, I'm not one of those classic people who would feel comfortable with children, who children crowd around and say, "Oh, do tell us a story," you know, and they have to be dragged away. Like Edward Lear was reputed to have you know, been—children fell in droves at his feet, kind of thing. I'm not . . .

**You didn't seem different from other kids?**

No.

**You made up stories of epilepsy in an interview once.**

Oh, I did that. I'm sure everybody must do that—throw epileptic fits on buses. I think that's a standard thing, when you're about twelve or thirteen.

**Do you think the first books people read are maybe as influential as anything else in their lives? If I had to guess which the early books you read were, from just seeing your work, I might have included *Dracula* in there.**

That's one of the first books I remember reading. As were the *Alice* books, about the same time.

**I suppose if your first books had been *Winnie the Pooh* and *Hans Brinker*, you'd have been working for Hallmark Cards now.**

Well, *Winnie the Pooh* was one of the first books I read, too.

**You're a self-taught reader?**

Yes.

**How is that possible?**

Don't ask me. I've always wondered how people learn to read, because I learned to read when I was about three and a half. And the only thing anybody says is, occasionally I would ask somebody what a word was in a newspaper or a book. Nobody, apparently, tried to teach me, I mean, nobody taught me. I had learned to read before anybody thought of doing it.

**When did you first lift a drawing pen?**

At the age of one and a half. My mother has treasured little drawings. My grandparents lived in a suburb of Chicago which overlooked

**"Sausage Train," the earliest known drawing by Edward Gorey**

the Northwestern Railroad, a very small town called Winthrop Harbor. It's on the border between Illinois and Wisconsin, actually. It wasn't really a suburb then—it was quite separate.

**And who put a pen in your hand?**

Oh, I suppose it was a pencil, actually.

**You grabbed it and began to—**

These very funny little sausagey drawings, which are meant to be railway cars.

**You studied French literature at Harvard.**

At Harvard, yes.

**Why French and not English?**

I figured I'd read everything I wanted to read in English, but I would have to force myself to read all of French literature. And I thought I would like to read all of French literature. It turned out Harvard had a perfectly god-awful French department at the period. And most of my survey courses used to come right after lunch, in which I would have a nice nap, so that my French is. . . . And many years later, I thought, "My god. I read about one French book a year. This is a great waste of my education." So I went out and bought lots of French books, but that's about the extent of it.

**Can we have a look at *The Deranged Cousins* now?**

[Cavett shows the pictures and reads the story, in which three cousins who live together on the edge of a salt marsh meet their ends. One brains another with a brown china doorknob in a quarrel over a bed slat they found in the marsh, a second dies after drinking a bottle of contaminated vanilla extract, while the third is swept away by an "unusually high tide."]

That story, unlikely as it seems, was taken from life.

**Well, I thought that was a put-on. When someone asked you once "Why do you constantly do murder, and bodies discovered, and so on?" you said, "I like to work from life."[1] What is the genesis of *The Deranged Cousins*?**

I spend half the year up on Cape Cod. And whatever the year that I did [the book]—I've forgotten now—but one Labor Day weekend, my two cousins and myself took a walk, you know, which this resulted in. Needless to remark, nothing happened after we took the walk—we went home again.

**Oh, I see.**

But the decor and sort of the details were, you know, picked up that day, as it were. The bed slat, and the doorknob, and the bottle of vanilla extract were all, you know, real objects lying around.

**There was no deceased involved?**

Oh, no, no, no, no.

**At least, so far as we're going to be told.**

My cousins are —

**Alive and kicking.**

—alive and kicking, yes.

**I have to tell you that I have total admiration for your work. And I think, also, for your lifestyle—that dreadful phrase.**

I agree about that.

**The idea that you live exactly as you want to. You do, apparently, a very satisfying kind of work. I find it just marvelous to look at, but I can imagine that it must be wonderful to do. I may be wrong about that. And I'm talking, also, about the fact that if you want to go to the ballet fifty nights in a row, you do; if you want to live in a house full of cats, you do; if your work isn't ready by the time the publisher wants it to be, apparently this doesn't get you terribly upset. And of the thousands and thousands of kinds of lives there are to lead, most people opt for one or two of the best-known ones. And you have done exactly, as I see it, what you want to do.**

Well, I guess I have. But only because I didn't really see any way of doing anything else.

**But when you were in the Army, did they say, "What are you gonna be, Gorey? You better shape up!"?**

No, I was one of those people who sort of slithered through the Army. For one thing, I always felt I was fortunate being in the Army during World War II, rather than, you know, later—say, during, well, Korea or Vietnam.

**The more ambiguous wars.**

Yeah, the more ambiguous ones. I mean, as it was, everybody was in the Army when I was in the Army, during the war. I spent most of my time being a company clerk ninety miles from Salt Lake City, in the desert. That terrible place where they—well, remember that George C. Scott movie about the poison gas?

**Oh, yes.**

"The Rage," I believe it was called or something. But anyway, that was based on the place I was—the Dugway Proving Ground, which I believe is still there. And every time I pick up a paper and see, you know, that 12,000 more sheep died mysteriously out in Utah, I think, "Oh, they're at it again."

**What influence should an art scholar see in your work? What painters?**

Mostly what it is, is 19th-century wood and steel engraved illustration—you know, not by anyone particular. Well, Doré[2] I've always liked a lot, but I wasn't particularly conscious of Doré as one particular artist until long after my own style had been set. I was always rather fascinated by that kind of thing. Well, it's the same thing that fascinated Max Ernst,[3] I guess. Just that kind of funny quality that emerged. Which isn't really artistic or anything, because it was, after all, done by hack engravers and things, with these tools. You know, I don't think anybody can do it anymore.

You know, you look at the original drawings for *Alice in Wonderland* that Tenniel[4] did, which are just wash drawings, rather than engravings. So that the Dalziel brothers,[5] or however you pronounce them, are really responsible, in a sense, for the quality of the Tenniel drawings. For instance, those funny square-toed feet that turn up in the *Alice* are not Tenniel—they're the Dalziel brothers. Because in every single thing that they ever engraved, no matter by whom, those square feet turn up.

**In your drawings, many of the toes turn out, as in ballet.**

Ballet. It's not so much conscious, but I think I realized early on that one of the things that makes ballet what it is, is that it's the maximum of expressiveness. I mean the sides of the feet, you know, the sides— and, you know, obviously, when your legs are turned out they're well, like Egyptian art or something. You know, each piece is the way it's most expressive: the profile, the profiles of the legs, the front of the torso, the front of the hands, and stuff. And so is ballet, I think. Somewhere along the line I obviously began to realize that I was being influenced by ballet. And it probably, you know, worked both ways since everybody draws himself.

But as I began to copy my own drawings, I'd get a little more bizarre. And then, you know, then I'd start copying myself as I looked, as I had, you know, gotten more and more stylized. And you obviously get very self-conscious, eventually, which is, I think, one of the things you have to be aware of.

**My wife has a friend who is forty-third on a waiting list for *The Beastly Baby*, which is one of your things, like the one based on the Moors Murders, which, I gather, a lot of bookstores refused to show because it was just too gruesome.**

I never could get it published. That was how I started publishing myself. I thought, "Oh I've been sitting around looking at this stupid little thing for many years." "Waste not, want not" was always my motto, so I founded The Fantod Press.

***Dracula*, which you do on Broadway—you did the designs for—has somewhat been eclipsed by your being in it, if you know what I mean. I mean, every review has—it's called *Edward Gorey's Dracula*, for one thing. And the reviewers seem to begin by talking about the sets, which is one of the first times in theatrical history, I think.**

Which I find very strange, because after all, I mean, I've been sitting around for twenty-five years, doing books. And this is the first time I've ever ventured into—

**—the Big Street?**

—the Big Street. And suddenly, it—you know, I just don't really understand it. I suppose, at the time it arrived. And it wouldn't much have mattered . . .

**I'm sorry. Had you finished that sentence?**

I guess I'd finished—yes. I actually tend to be very inconsequential and trail off.

**When you saw your drawings blown up to that terrific great proportion that they are in the play, did it become other than Gorey for you?**

I practically had cardiac arrest, is what I practically had.

**How so?**

Well, I don't know. I was prepared. I'd seen things blown up before. I felt the scale of the—the main thing—I felt was wrong. And since nobody else agrees with me, there's no point in belaboring the point. I felt the scale was wrong, that I should have done them on a larger scale. I don't like blown-up drawing very much.

**If you'd known they were going to be that big, you'd have done the originals in a different scale?**

Well, no. I knew they were going to be that big and everything, but as it was . . . See, I had originally done that design of *Dracula* for Nantucket back in 1973, for this stage that was not much bigger than this thing. And I had done it on a much smaller scale there and it had worked all right, because it was a very dark little pocket type stage. But when I saw this—I just felt the drawing, for my purpose, for my taste, everything was much too open. But, on the other hand, I don't think they could have probably executed the sets if I'd done them on a much larger scale—it would have been too costly. So . . .

**There is something very important in the books about the scale of your works. It seems to me it's easier to enter that weird world in that small size than it would be blown up. We have a *Dracula* poster. [Shows poster.] Do you have any particular feeling for or against bats?**

Oh, I'm rather fond of bats, I think.[6] I've never had one, you understand.

**I've petted a bat. Were you at all influenced by the Lugosi film images? And did you have to shed any influence?**

No. I don't suppose I've seen the Lugosi film[7] for, gosh, I don't know how many years. It's one of my favorite movies. When I started doing this I wasn't particularly conscious, you know, of antecedent. Or I don't remember thinking about it one way or the other.

**No problem for you.**

No. Well, somehow, when we got talking about the set, it had to be a certain way because of such and such. And we, you know, invented these five arches, with the plugs that fill them and change the set. There obviously must be something that has crept into that set that I didn't put there, as it were.

**Actors.**

Well, that. But, I mean, the fact that everybody has reviewed the sets—which I don't think is entirely just because I—I'm obviously not that well enough known so that it's exactly all that much of an event that I'm asked to do a play on Broadway. So I think some kind of monumentality crept into the set, which I wasn't prepared for. But that's nice, because if something doesn't creep into a drawing that you're not prepared for, you might just as well not have drawn it, I think.

**The creeping in is somehow important.**

Yeah.

**Well, I certainly enjoyed meeting you. And I congratulate you on the fact that you dressed and lived this way before it was fashionable. You've been somewhat camouflaged into the background now.**

Well, I'm being caught up with. And now I'm going to recede slowly down the . . .

**The only way you could be as different as you were in the '50s now would be to wear a suit and tie constantly.**

Yes. I mean, it's a little late, I feel.

# The Cat Quotes
of Edward Gorey

Jane Merrill Filstrup,
*Cats Magazine*, May 1978

"Cats share with ballet dancers the quality of graceful movement. As an artist, I find their expressions endlessly and frustratingly fascinating. Every now and again I'll do a quick sketch of my cats, but I draw very badly from life. Has a cat ever posed for me? Not posed would be more like it. He or she usually moves the instant [I get] the idea of sketching same, even if it has previously been comatose for hours."

The speaker was Edward Gorey, an artist whose miniature novels are masterpieces of peculiar whimsy. What follows are Edward Gorey's unique thoughts on cats and people and how they live together:

66    JANE MERRILL FILSTRUP

"I got my first cat when I was about seven. Apart from when I was at Harvard and in the Army, I've always had cats, all of them shorthairs. I can't conceive of life without cats. I don't believe I've ever forgotten any cat I had, even if circumstances conspired that I only had it for a short time. On the other hand, I don't have too many specific memories of them, but then I don't have many specific memories of people who are no longer around either.

"For years, I used to try to keep their number down to three, because of my one-room apartment. But then, as one does, I knew other people with cats. You find a cat on the street and try to foist it off on somebody else. My various blackmailing ventures like that have come home to roost. People will call me and say, 'Listen, we don't like to bother you, but we've got this cat. And if you don't take it, we're going to put it in the oven.' So, though I live on the same street as Bide-a-Wee, I've never had cause to stop in. And following more than one of these ventures, I ended up with six.

"Between three and four, before I took in the fifth, didn't seem much difference. Between four and five didn't seem much difference. Strangely enough, between five and six I suddenly felt it's not just six cats, it's six cats making up a kind of phalanx. Not that the six banded together. To the contrary, there were all sorts of internecine relationships. But somehow six cats seem a lot more, disproportionately more, than five. I lost one this spring, so now I'm down to five, which once more is five individuals.

"I name them whatever strikes me at the time. The names usually turn out to be wildly unsuitable. For example, Agrippina couldn't be less like the original (wife of the emperor Claudius; Nero's mother). Most of their names are from *The Tale of Genji* by Lady Murasaki. At present I feel *Genji* is inexhaustible, though obviously when the name is hard to pronounce, un-Japanese nicknames creep in. The cats all have about six nicknames.

"The Abyssinian, going on seventeen, was given to me by friends who had her mother, a perplexing cat, quite indescribable. She was very pretty. Who has ever seen an Abyssinian who wasn't? But she seemed to have absolutely no character. She wasn't shy, she wasn't outgoing, she wasn't withdrawn, she wasn't happy, she wasn't sad, she wasn't anything—she was just *there*. When they offered me a kitten I said, 'Oh, I'm not sure.' They realized exactly what I was intimating. 'Oh listen,' they said, 'we'll give you the kitten that has personality.' And indeed she does. She's diminutive. She's all personality and crazed charm. She's spent her whole life torn between being incredibly shy and incredibly friendly. You can watch her go into paroxysms of 'Shall I run up the bookcase and disappear; or shall I come over and talk to somebody?' She learned to purr when she was ten years old. She was always affectionate with me, but her purring was delayed. Now of course she never stops and she's become more friendly than she used to be.

"The most intelligent cat I've ever had was twelve in August. Kanzuke is a brilliant cat, very friendly and emotionally distressed. When worked up, he bites and scratches. He feuds with one of his sisters. Occasionally I inadvertently get so upset by this I try to separate them. I once had a number of holes up and down one arm—little white craters which took months to heal. The other arm had claw marks from upper arm to wrist. Those healed rather rapidly. Once he bit me so hard I had to have a tetanus shot. My whole wrist swelled up in half a minute.

"The house my cousins and I have at the Cape is at the head of a marina, where Koko had been living on boats. She has one black-ribbed eye, one orange-ribbed eye. There are still stray cats, well-fed ones, abroad in Barnstable, who are related to Koko. She is very sweet and she purrs a lot, but [is] totally brainless as far as I can gather. She's never shown the slightest sign of intelligence. She's very domestic looking and enormous.

"To No Chun is a pale ginger cat, very long, thin and bony. This one I felt sorry for at the vet's one day, and adopted. My vet always has a cage on display. I was talking to him about the ginger cat, without any intention of taking it. Then the vet said, 'Anybody who takes that cat had better see beforehand how badly crippled it is.' 'Oooh, poor little thing, what is the matter with him? I'll take him. I'll take him,' I said, figuring nobody else would. He'd fallen or been pushed off a terrace.

His back leg had been broken and twisted so that when sitting up one back leg would stick out. He has worn all the fur off the back of it because of the odd way he has to sit down. He'd been inside the cage for a couple of days already. When they dumped him out, he slithered along the floor. I thought, 'Oh my God, what have I done? My other cats will kill him because he's not agile and fast like the others.' I took him home anyway, expecting he wouldn't be able to get up on anything. Well, he is a perfect demon. I think what he did was—he didn't fall off the terrace, he probably sailed off it, in a great fit of euphoria. He wants to sit on my shoulder all the time. He flings himself up. I'm glad I took him in because he's a sweet cat and a peacemaker, compatible with the other four.

"If you have just one cat, it tends to fade when the owner is not around. But among several cats—though mine seem to sleep a great deal of the day, too—there is a complex of relationships going on. One cat will allow the other cats to sleep up against it. There's also a pecking order, which is funny to watch. Kanzuke has ruled the house for years and years, although a couple of the lady cats will occasionally assert themselves. Agrippina is bullied by everybody, but once a year she runs amok—'I'm not having any more of this'—and she sets to skirmishing with everybody, a situation lasting about a week. Kanzuke tries to bully Stubbs, but Stubbs will have nothing to do with it. He lays his ears back and shuts his eyes, sitting still as a statue, which nonplusses Kanzuke. They're actually fond of each other. Koko is basically indifferent to the others, but amiable. Stubbs and Maude like each other quite well. Agrippina makes friends, but she is sometimes pushed from the food dish, the poor dear.

"Days when I'm at home they may pay me no attention at all. Which is better than the days when they decide they all want to sit on the drawing-board, no matter what I'm doing. Sometimes there is the full complement of five of them draped on the drawing-board, and there used to be six. They slither to the center and put their claws out to attract my notice.

"None of my cats go out-of-doors at all, even at the Cape. In Murray Hill, it's no ledge nonsense for me—I'm far too neurotic about it. Though they have their times for looking out the windows, the cats don't seem to do it excessively, or enough to make me feel guilty they are in one room. Indoor cats don't lose their wildness, which is one reason I am so fascinated by them. They seem to retain all their jungly qualities no matter what."

# An Interview with Edward St. John Gorey at the Gotham Book Mart

Jane Merrill Filstrup,

*The Lion and the Unicorn*, Number I, 1978

A tall man of noble Viking countenance, bearded, a gold stud in one earlobe, and on brumal days, wearing a floor-length fur coat:

**Do you think there's any similarity among passionate admirers of your work?**

The question of audience. I have no idea. I see no common denominator. The readers range from small children to tottery elderly folk like myself. In some cases it doesn't even mean much sophistication. Lately

**Edward Gorey at the Gotham Book Mart, New York**
*Photographer: Bill Yoscary*

I've been receiving letters from people who have known my work for a long time. "Oh Mr. Gorey, do keep yourself recherché." And I think, "That's all very well for you to talk." They think they discovered me way back and resist the idea of the world's moving in.

**But that's a natural response. Your work gives the impression of having been written for a coterie of friends.**

I wouldn't even say that. Basically I've written what I've written because it's the only mode in which I can write or draw. It stands to reason that friends like my work, but I don't write for them any more than for others. Some authors are aware of what their audience is like and what the audience wants. I haven't a clue.

**So the manuscripts usually come first?**

Invariably. I discovered very early that without the manuscript absolutely complete I can't do the book. If I were to begin drawing sooner than that, everything would fall to pieces. Some of my manuscripts I've written in an afternoon. Others are partial for years. Suddenly I'll think about a story, take it up, and either finish it or do more work on it. Endless numbers of unfinished ones sit there waiting.

**What is your typical day's work schedule?**

Oh, I manage to pull myself together after breakfast. I can work very well at night, but hate doing it, because then I stay awake all night. Whatever I gained the night before is dissipated the following day. I tend to try to work in the morning and in the early afternoon. Say for a week or so I can work eight hours a day. But that has to stop after a while, because I become strung up.

**Does your pattern of work differ at Barnstable on the Cape from in Manhattan?**

No, it boils down to the same thing. I have endless numbers of distractions in both places. Even the cats are there, climbing on to the drawing board in both places. It just happens that the distractions are completely undomestic in New York. I'm out every night at the ballet or the opera or concerts. While at the Cape I scarcely ever go out. I cook for the family up there. The thought of going out for a meal—we couldn't possibly—whereas here I never have a meal in, partly because I have an awful one-room apartment with a little Pullman kitchen. If you cook anything, you can smell it three weeks later. I'm afraid I can be distracted wherever I am by something.

**You began writing in a culturally barren environment, in the desert of Utah during your Army stint.**

I always wonder what I thought I was doing then, because what I was writing was clearly unpresentable—closet dramas, for instance. I had very little sense of purpose, which was just as well, because then I wasn't disappointed about the outcome.

**Would you talk a bit about your childhood drawings and writings?**

My first drawing was of the trains that used to pass by my grandparents' house, done at age three and a half.[1] The composition was of various sausage shapes. There was a sausage for the railway car, sausages for the wheels, and little sausages for the windows. I didn't start writing seriously until I was in the Army.

**Did you ever keep a journal?**

Lord no. I envy people who do. After a few years they have an abundance of material to draw upon.

**Have decisions to use black and white been based on the economics of the books?**

I've had a natural tendency toward black and white anyway. At one point I wanted to paint, but that was when I was very young. Line drawing is where my talent lies. I do work in color and like to, to some extent. But the preference for black and white was confirmed [when I worked] at Doubleday. I immediately became aware that it is much easier to have a black-and-white book accepted, especially since it seemed they would never publish my books as literature for children. My training caused me to be very conscious of what constituted a book, so I have always been very careful in coordinating the parts of my books, putting them together. I naturally think in terms of how many pages there will be, how the pages turn, and so forth.

**In addition to the books you have illustrated by other authors, when have you written specifically for children?**

When I first started out, I wasn't trying to write for children because I didn't know any children. Then again, I mean "knowing" in the fashion of people who talk to the kiddies all the time. This simply would not work for me. However, I have thought that more of my work might have been for children than anybody would ever publish on a juvenile list. *The Doubtful Guest* was for children, by my estimation. I used to try to persuade a publisher by saying, "Why don't you bring this out as a children's book? I have an adult audience which will buy the book anyway. You might as well pick up some children along the line." But they would not risk it, they'd get all twittery. So I gave up.

**When you were a child, would you have relished *The Gashlycrumb Tinies*?**

Probably, yes. I was reading very early. I taught myself when I was about three and a half, and read just everything. I read *Alice* and

*Dracula* the same month, I guess, at between five and seven. There was no one to stop me from reading anything that I could lay my hands on, so I read comic books, and the collected works of Victor Hugo when I was eight—a feat I could not repeat now. I've always liked horror stories. My parents were great detective readers, and I've been reading detective stories as long as I can remember.

**The children in your books suffer a great deal. Do you think of childhood as a period of misery?**

For some people it is. I'm sure mine was happier than I imagine in retrospect. I look back and think, "Oh poetic me," but it simply was not true. I was out playing Kick-the-Can along with everyone else.

**Do you expect a reaction of compassion to the children's cruel fates?**

I aim to provoke a level of non-emotional response, as well as to keep myself distant. One of my most popular books is *The Hapless Child*, which I've always felt is excessive—although I can't say what I would treat differently doing the story now.

**Too close to the lachrymose tales it parodies?**

Overdone is the best way I can put it.

**What were your early experiences of death?**

My first cat died when I was very small. We had a couple of dogs: one got run over. That I remember being very upset by. We had the dog for only a month, but it was a very nice dog. He died chasing a squirrel. We lived in the suburbs and he was hit by a car and was put out of the way. Our second cat was poisoned after we had it for about six months. As far as deaths in the intimate family or among close friends, there have never been many. I lost quite a few relatives, but I do not recall being traumatized as a child.

Despite this sudden change of fate,
She soon began to perorate.

**What children's responses have filtered to you about the books?**

Some fan letters come from children. It's hard to see what children get from books. What did I make of *Dracula* when I was five or seven? I recall being very scared by it, but certainly missed a lot. People have come to me and said, "My child just adores *The Curious Sofa*." At first this baffled me, but apparently they find it funny. Maybe the humor for them derives from the repetition of certain words and phrases. For example, I purposely made personal names in *The Curious Sofa* practically indistinguishable one from the other. And there are gimmicks to

The simple creature was aghast
At hearing of her cruel past.

flatten the prose, like the constant reiteration of the "well-endowed young man." A kind of poetry may come through to the child even though the phrase was put in as a parody on pornography where everybody is faceless, undifferentiated.

**Do you have any favorites among better-known European fairy tales?**

Fairy tales disturb me somewhat. A rational part of my mind rejects them. We all rewrite them in our heads, according to our fancies. Take *The Frog Prince*. The frog changes into a prince at the moment when that princess, an awfully uppity little bitch—of course who remembers that?—hurls it against the wall trying to kill it. Fairy tales may be incomprehensible to the individual. They have grown that way. No one mind cast them as they exist. Even Perrault[1] was a codifier. So they express collective truths, as Bruno Bettelheim's book[2] points up. I do admire the funny, irrational quality of fairy tales. That is one of my fascinations. What if one were to write a completely rational "fake" fairy tale? And there's one Grimm fairy tale I'd like to illustrate. I've worked it out perfectly as one of my thirty drawings books. It's two tales stuck together, called *Clever Alice.* The story begins with a courtship. The girl goes down to the cellar for beer. "Suppose the axe fell from the ceiling onto the head of my child," she says. The family and the suitor join her one by one, 'til pretty soon everyone has collected in the cellar and they're weeping and wailing. The second part takes place after the pair are married. The wife goes out into the fields to reap corn. She falls asleep, and not knowing who she is, the husband throws a net over her head. On her return she knocks on the door and the husband answers. But he says his wife is already in the house. "Then who am I?" she asks, and wanders off. There is much to draw: people descending into the cellar in this cumulative effect, the spooky business of "who am I?" Walter Crane drew only one picture for each Grimm story in his edition, so great scope is left to work it up into a book.

**How did you happen to write the *Fletcher and Zenobia* books, which were illustrated by another author?**

Victoria Chess had written a version expressly so that she could illustrate it. She took it to Peter Weed at Dodd, Mead, who is also my editor. He loved the drawings but felt the text was unsatisfactory. So they asked me to write her a text. I kept the plot but transformed Zenobia from a human being into a doll. It was too spooky having a real live person hatched from an egg. Vicky's drawings were beautiful but she was hopelessly dissatisfied with them all, so she redrew the entire book. I'm supposed to do a third *Fletcher and Zenobia* book. I outlined it five years ago, but haven't begun writing.

**How do you handle collaborations?**

On the whole, I enjoy collaborating with people. They usually produce the text, and I do the drawings without consulting them.

**Will you continue illustrating other people's books, or is that kind of partnership over?**

Not at all. I plan to do *Alice's Adventures in Wonderland* and *Through the Looking Glass* for Putnam, eventually, a project I anticipate with a great deal of alarm. Sometime I would very much like to illustrate Daisy Ashford's *The Young Visiters*, which came out around the end of the First World War. It is a late-Victorian novel Daisy Ashford wrote when she was about seven, but it was found much later in the attic of her family.[3] No grown-up could have written it. It has a loony tone which no other fiction I've ever read quite has, and was published complete with misspellings. It was written by a very bright child who had somehow penetrated to the heart of all the clichés of social behavior and presentation. Several illustrated editions have appeared, but because of this funny tone I've always felt I could do a good job on it. Then there's another novel which I began to illustrate years ago called *Irene Iddesleigh*, by a lady named Amanda M'Kittrick Ros.[4] She was an Irish washerwoman—to put it at its lowest level. Mrs. Ros wrote her novels in the purplest prose ever written. They are unreadable if you try to sit down and read straight through. They are Victorian novels of passion and crime, retribution and revenge. No one with a literary background could have achieved the utterly peculiar prose style of *Irene Iddesleigh*.

Trying to do a parody you'd fall down immediately. But she was totally sincere. Again, it's the odd tone which appeals to me.

**Are you ever bored by having to draw the same character over and over again in a book?**

No, that doesn't bother me, though it amazes me how cartoonists do their figures *ad infinitum*. No, it's mostly just how I must cover this much territory—augh. I've started on a background of wallpaper, for instance, and then realized how intricate the design was. You see, I feel all my people look alike. I merely use a few physical characteristics, like the clothes they're wearing, to distinguish them from one another.

**You once mentioned having copied your own drawing style to perfect it. You pointed out that this was a dangerous practice. Can you explain the danger?**

There is a tendency, if you have an idiosyncratic style, which obviously I do—I wish it weren't quite so identifiable but that is how it always works out—to fall into self-parody. However, since I never look at my stuff after I've finished it, I may have repeated myself unknowingly.

**How consciously do you borrow?**

It's conscious in a way of appreciation. Unfortunately, we live in a period when eclecticism has run amok. But I see no way of limiting it. I have a strong sense of imitation. I'm terrible at it, luckily. I recall taking courses in creative writing at Harvard when we were assigned to do pastiche. My pastiches turned out to be quite entertaining, but bore no relation to Pope or Dryden or whomever I was supposed to be imitating. They all ended up sounding like me. So I can afford to indulge this kind of exercise, filch blatantly from all over the place, because it will ultimately be mine. As someone once said, originality is not taking from somebody else. It's when nobody can take it from you and repeat it.

**Your plots are generally either inconclusive, or stop dead in a comic or ironic vein.**

I put a high value on plot as a kind of scaffolding. Underneath everything in my books is a lot of plot which holds them together. I'd love to be able to write Victorian novels with all the trimmings. I couldn't do it. But I do try to construct a strong plot, at least in the books that are not merely compilations like the alphabet.

I like literature to be either very short or very long. What I dislike is writing which is very exhaustive. Thomas Mann tells everything there is to know, leaving virtually nothing to the imagination. "Good grief," I think. Trollope, whom I adore, is far more solid. Solidity is the quality I admire most in fiction—the quality that makes you feel these are real people, authentic situations. Of course this does not apply precisely to my work. Nevertheless, I try to make my work solid. My ideal is Jane Austen. She represents to me the most solid person in English literature. And I like Japanese literature very much. It is amorphic, with drift, with fluctuation in everything, but with an ineffable reality beneath it all, whereas Thomas Mann seems to me exhaustive without being convincing.

**Which novels of Dickens do you like? Do any of his child characters stand out for you?**

My favorite Dickens tend to be the sinister bits. I love the idea of the Old Curiosity Shop, or of Little Nell and her grandfather. There is no earthly reason why Quilp shouldn't have caught up with them on page twelve. What's marvelous about their flight is that it works. They are elusive until the end. My favorite single Dickens is probably *Our Mutual Friend* because it's so scary. I enjoy *Bleak House* and, too, *Great Expectations*—with Miss Havisham brooding in the cobwebbed room.

**What appeals to you about the E. F. Benson Lucia[5] books?**

I inadvertently discovered the "Lucia" books in 1943, when I was in the Army. There is an omnibus edition of them in print now. If I were driven to decide what to take along to a desert island, it would be a toss-up among Jane Austen's complete works, *The Tale of Genji*, the "Lucia" books, or one of the Trollope series. Regrettably, I've read the "Lucia" books so often I almost know them by heart, so there's little incentive to reread them.

**Are you a fan of thrillers?**

Yes, especially Agatha Christie. I've read all her books at least once. When she died, I thought, "This is the end!"

**Some of your work has been called surrealistic. Do you view yourself in the Surrealist tradition?**

Yes. That philosophy appeals to me. I mean that is my philosophy if I have one, certainly in the literary way. On the other hand, most Surreal art strikes me as very boring indeed, although Max Ernst's collages are wonderful. I suspect that the kind of thing I do is just the kind of thing that drives me crazy in other authors. I like the Surrealism of Charles Cros,[6] whose piece I illustrated—*The Salt Herring*—in *Amphigorey Too*. I also translated Alphonse Allais'[7] monologue, *Le Hareng saur* (*Story for Sara*). His is pre-Surrealist art, I suppose. I sit reading André Breton and think, "Yes, yes, you're so right." What appeals to me most is an idea expressed by Eluard.[8] He has a line about there being another world, but it's in this one. And Raymond Queneau[9] said the world is not what it seems—but it isn't anything else, either. These two ideas are the bedrock of my approach. If a book is only what it seems to be about, then somehow the author has failed.

**What about the Surrealist doctrine that a writer conjures without fully understanding the work and sees more meaning in it after the fact?**

That is one of the thorniest questions. Take, for instance, Henry James, my favorite bête noire. Sometimes I think he knows perfectly well what he writes about, as in *Turn of the Screw*, and is quite brilliant. Other times he unnerves me. I think, "Henry, did you realize what this was about when you wrote it? You've been going on for several hundred pages and apparently have no idea what you're saying." For example, I don't believe James ever realized how detestable the behavior of the characters is in *The Aspern Papers*. Even more so *The Figure in the Carpet*, where a famous novelist says there's a figure in the carpet of his work which no one has ever discerned. A woman goes to the length of marrying him to learn the secret. When the author dies, a critic marries her to find out. The motivation is totally insane: utterly unpleasant arid curiosity. Yet James goes blithely on, seemingly unaware how loathsome these people appear to any person not a monster to begin with. That story is a classic example of unconscious writing.

**Your early works like *The Beastly Baby* seem more outrageous than your later books. Is that merely stylistic shift or do you feel that you're mellowing?**

Oh, I think, "Why bother?" For one thing, it's exceedingly hard to outrage anybody anymore, given the state of the world. And I truly am more interested in what everyday life is like. People think I think everyday life is filled with murder. But to me every day is completely different from every other day, even when nothing at all is happening. That is what has always appealed to me about Japanese literature. It has a stronger sense of what life is to the individual living it than any other literature I've ever read. *The Tale of Genji* displays subtleties of feeling about existence rarely dealt with in Western literature.

# The Mind's Eye:
# Writers Who Draw

Jean Martin,

*Drawing*, July–August 1980

Edward Gorey sent some written answers to a number of questions about his drawing procedures:

"I have to have the finished text of a book before I start on the drawings; on the occasions when I tried starting on the drawings before, no book resulted; I don't know why. The germ of a book, however, may be either visual or verbal.

"As to materials . . . virtually everything is done on Strathmore two-ply matt finish. For years I used Hunt #204 penpoints and Higgins India ink; somewhere along the line I switched to Gillotts

*B was a Bore who engaged him in talk*

B was a Bore who engaged him in talk

titquill penpoints and Pelikan ink. When Gillotts titquills disappeared, I went with reluctance back to Hunt #104. None of these—paper, pen, and ink—seem to be what they once were, so I expect I am getting old.

"Any preliminary drawings I do are of the roughest, sometimes thumbnails of the whole book which only I could make out. There is some preliminary pencil drawing on the drawing itself, but this is also

fairly rough, and there is only anything more elaborate and meticulous when it involves something overall like wallpaper or some complicated object, e.g., an automobile, which I am filching from somewhere else. I really can't say anything about how I develop an idea or a drawing to the final stages because I haven't any idea.

"All my drawings are done to the size of reproduction, the only exception being when the final result is going to be more than, say, six inches in any direction, then I work smaller and have it blown up, because I am uncomfortable working any larger unless I absolutely have to.

"I correct drawings only in a very minor way—with white tempera and/or a razor blade. In desperation I may redraw a segment and paste it over if I feel unable to redo the rest of the drawing as well a second time.

"I don't have a studio, at least not so's you could notice. In New York I have a one-room apartment which by the window has a drafting table and a taboret; on Cape Cod in my attic bedroom I have a kitchen table at one end of it. My drawing space is not arranged, if only because anywhere from one to six cats are almost always sitting on wherever I am working. Also, I have never understood how artists can bear to be surrounded by their own work. Mine goes out of sight as soon as it is finished and is in most cases never really looked at again.

"I don't use models, at least not actual ones except very, very seldom. I do a lot of filching, however, from all over the place. (I cannot sufficiently repay Dover for all they have supplied me with.) Clothes are sometimes researched, or were once, and sometimes made up, undoubtedly from past recollections for the most part.

"My first drawings date back to the age of one and a half. Yes, but I think without displaying any particular talent. My art training was negligible; again I don't think I displayed any particular talent. Why I have kept on drawing all these years I can't imagine; probably because I never thought of anything else to do.

"From 1953 until my first show at Graham Gallery, whenever that was,[1] I did no drawing that was not intended for a book, and from 1953 I have never done any drawing at all for my own pleasure. It somehow never occurred to me. I do work in color from time to time—watercolored drawings rather than watercolors; my seeming predilection for black and white is partially accountable to the fact that I knew from the beginning it was almost impossible to get my sort of book published in color on account of the expense, and eventually I ended up thinking in black and white.

"The fact that I *draw* in the typeface in the books is an accident. I did a couple of sample pages, hand-lettered, for my second book, *The Listing Attic*, to show how it would look, and they, the publishers thought what a good idea hand-lettering was, and since then I have never been able to stop; I sometimes get *fearfully* bored lettering the damn things, especially since I really detest my hand-lettering.

"Painters I admire: La Tour, Piero della Francesca, Uccello, Matisse, Vuillard, Bonnard, Balthus, Bacon, Burchfield. Writers: Jane Austen, Lady Murasaki, Anthony Trollope, the 'Lucia' books of E. F. Benson. Illustrators: three Edwards—Lear, Bawden, Ardizzone.[2]

"In my case, my mind's eye, and for that matter, ear, if you take that as a symbol or whatever for the verbal or writing part, if it/they exist, they do so on a completely unconscious level. I have no conscious visual imagination whatever, or at least I have no idea what the drawing will look like until it is done, which is just as well, because I would be so depressed by the difference between ideal and real that I would proba-bly have never started drawing at all as a regular thing. When I do have to try and visualize before drawing for one reason or another—perhaps an illustration that has to have a certain number of elements in it—I tend to become paralyzed, and the results are usually terrible. In other words, I suppose, since I do not draw from life, I manage to function by suppressing any consciousness of my mental images until they are on paper; I know that over the years I have found the things that came the easiest and that I didn't have to think about at all were the ones that worked out the best. Anything that really had to be fussed over was probably not worth the effort."

# Edward Gorey

Lisa Solod,

*Boston Magazine*, September 1980

Edward Gorey greeted my arrival in Hyannis with a warm smile and a jovial hello, even though my bus was an hour late (he passed the time reading Agatha Christie). He was dressed in faded blue jeans, white tennis shoes, and a pair of heavy gold earrings in the shape of lions' heads. Gorey is a handsome man who looks like a cross between Ernest Hemingway and Santa Claus. He has a long, tangled bluish beard and soft, short grey-white hair. His eyes are Paul Newman–blue, icy at first glance, but filled with charm and humor. He is fifty-three years old and thinks he looks every bit of it. But it is hard to think of him as a man approaching old age, especially when he breaks into a light skip as he walks.

On both occasions, Gorey drove us to lunch in his battered 1972 Volkswagen—once at Turner's Ice Cream Parlor, where he spent the better part of an hour talking about the hit television series *Dallas* (he has memorized the plots to every show), *Star Trek*, and the British-import science fiction series, *Dr. Who*; the second time at Mildred's Chowder House, a Cape Cod institution, where we again exhaustively discussed *Dallas* and also *Being There*, which Gorey had just seen and enjoyed.

After lunch we went to the Barnstable house—a writer's dream of an abode; rooms upon rooms decorated with Gorey's beanbag toys, antiques, and old bargain-basement chairs and couches. It is comfortable and cozy. The attic where he summers is filled with books piled from floor to ceiling. A draft blows in through the windows, making it quite cold in winter, but very pleasant in summer. In the tiny back room is a small, narrow bed where Gorey sleeps, accompanied at any given moment by at least three of his cats.

The interviews took place around a small wooden table in Gorey's kitchen. We chatted for nearly five hours during both visits, over many cups of tea, Gorey sprinkling his conversation with many "you knows," great, throaty laughs, and huge body sighs. The view from the kitchen is of Barnstable Harbor—serene, clean, and extraordinarily beautiful. I saw quickly why Gorey has given up the hustle-bustle of New York City to stay there. The solitude is good for his writing; he does not get lonely. And although with his cheery, ruddy fisherman's face and casual dress, he looks every bit a Cape native, I wondered if Gorey—in his "declining years," as he calls them—thinks he has finally come home.

**Do you consider yourself a New Englander?**

Only by adoption.

**Are you accepted down here?**

I don't really know anyone here. I had more friends at one point than I do now; they've all moved away. At one time I did find myself becoming involved with people who lived in the country—usually in more remote places than the Cape—but they were very urban and sophisticated and all they would see were other very sophisticated people who lived in remote places. They were heavy drinkers: you go for cocktails at six and dinner at midnight. Relentless gossip. And everybody *does* something.

**Do you find country life claustrophobic?**

I remember when *Dracula* opened on Nantucket so many years ago; I went over for the day. I got a glimpse of what life on that island is like. You go to someone's house and he says, "Oh, I see you didn't take the milk in until quarter after seven this morning. Usually you take it in at quarter of."

**You keep your distance because you don't want people prying into your business?**

My life is pure as the driven snow.

**So you spend most of your time with your family? Do you have close family ties?**

Yes. My mother was in a nursing home down here for some time. She died two years ago in October. I couldn't possibly have looked after her, though, so I put her in a perfectly nice rest home. I think she actually liked it. She had a stroke when she was about eighty and her entire character changed. All her hypocritical love for humanity vanished. Any parent-child relationship has its sides, you know. With Mother I was always getting carried away. I'd say, "Oh, Mother, let's face it. You dislike me sometimes as much as I dislike you." "Oh, no dear," she'd say. "I've always loved you."

**But did she love your work?**

She *appreciated* it. But, poor dear, she had become very sour toward me in the last five years of her life. She was, however, lovely to everyone else.

**You are an only child?**

Yes. And in childhood I loved reading nineteenth-century novels in which the families had twelve kids. I think it's just as well, though, that I didn't have any brothers or sisters. I saw in my own family that my mother and her two brothers and two sisters were always fighting. And then my grandmother would go insane and disappear for long periods of time.

**Sounds like eccentricity might run in the family. How do you fit in?**

Oh, I've always been eccentric. Part of me is genuinely eccentric, part of me is a bit of a put-on. But I know what I'm doing. I don't think I do anything I don't want to do. If you're at all self-conscious, you realize perfectly well what you're doing—most of the time.

**What's the dividing line?**

Well, frankly, living by yourself with six cats is eccentric.

**What about your reputation for wearing fur coats and sneakers?**

That part is genuinely eccentric. I wouldn't do it if it wasn't the way I wanted to dress. But I'm very much aware that I could be a little more or a little less eccentric.

**The Cape doesn't strike me as particularly decadent, which is a word that has been used to describe you and your work. How do you feel about that?**

Decadent. Ohhhhhh. —I'm really terribly innocent. I guess, though, that my work is slightly decadent. I think, however, that it is less decadent than other people's.

**But what kind of people do you think your work appeals to?**

Chances are I am going to appeal to someone who was brought up in the city rather than someone who was brought up on a farm in North Dakota, although you do get some awfully decadent people on farms in North Dakota. And you know, there are a lot of kids who like my work who obviously don't—well, they might understand it, but they're obviously not going to get a lot of the references. To do that, you have to be reasonably well read in a funny way. Aware. I am fairly interested in all the arts, and I think I use all that stuff in my work. Anyway, I'm more aware of it when I'm working. I tend to spend a lot of time in a stupor, but on the other hand, I am sort of hyper-conscious of what is going on.

**Why can't you seem to get past, say, 1930 in your work? That's not your generation.**

No, it's before I was born.

**Does the repression of that era interest you? Do you feel repressed?**

I am probably terribly repressed. But we won't go into that.

**Why won't we?**

I think it's very boring. I was talking to someone the other day, and I was saying that I don't think it is possible not to be one's own generation; however, on the surface, my work harks back to the Victorian and Edwardian periods. Basically I am absolutely contemporary because there is no way not to be. I am dealing with contemporary concerns. You've *got* to be contemporary.

**Still, you aren't contemporary in the sense that you talk about sex and politics and drugs.**

Well, no, that's true.

**Are you interested in politics?**

No. I voted one time, for Stevenson, in 1952.[1] By the time I moved to New York, I did not want to go on jury duty, and I wasn't political anyway, so I never registered to vote.

**So much for politics. How involved are you in the arts? In other people's work? What do you think of your contemporaries?**

I think many of them are doing the same thing over and over again. I don't see many advances.

**Does art have to advance to be exciting?**

There is no such thing as the avant garde anymore. I don't think anyone has done anything new since the First World War. People must realize that someone else did it long before they did, and did it with a great deal more elegance and offhandedness. And then there are those who devote themselves to the vertical strip . . . I think that everyone has his thing that he does over and over. But, at the same time, there are ways of doing things that are more interesting than others.

**When you say "interesting," do you mean "new"?**

I mean to some extent unexpected.

**So your own books are interesting—by your own criteria, that is.**

They are to me, or I could not write them. They aren't expected. They twist and turn. It's hard to say they are about this or that.

I have a dumb theory that a creative piece of art is only interesting if it purports to be about something and is really about something else. Quite often when I write or draw, my work starts out as a parody and sometimes turns into a parody of something else. In other words, I take some sort of given, but by the time I'm finished with what I wanted it to be about, what I *really* wanted it to be about has crept into it. For example, that's why I like J. R. on *Dallas*. He's so mean you get angry at him. But you like him. There's pleasure in it, but it is disturbing. That's a good definition of interesting.

**Why write about murder?**

I've always been interested in true crime and detective stories. I think crime is interesting because you learn a million things about people's lives that you ordinarily would not have heard about; crazy details about the way people live.

**Are English crimes more exciting than American ones?**

There are better English crimes. And crime is better written about in England. In a sense, the more conventional a society is, the more interesting the crime. It's interesting to read about people who have nice houses and lots of money but who do terrible things.

**One senses a preoccupation with death running through a lot of your work. Do you fear death? Do you think about it often?**

I think about it constantly. Doesn't everyone?

**Why? Because there is still so much you have not done?**

I've been saying recently that I have passed from the post-college generation to old age with no interim period. Suddenly I feel that I am old, that the sunset years are right here. Where did my middle age go? I have had these protracted post-college years—for twenty-five years! That's where my middle age went to! —How do you define middle age anyway?

**They say it starts at forty. You're middle-aged.**

Well! —My most traumatic birthday was my thirtieth. I can still remember saying, "Help! I don't feel very well today!" And a friend said, "Well, dear, after thirty you have your good days and your bad days."

Actually, until I was well into my forties I looked as if I was in my late twenties. Now, however, I do look my age, if not older. But I would rather be that way than supernaturally well preserved.

**You do not share the contemporary obsession with fitness and appearance? With youth?**

Well, I only said that because I do not look supernaturally well preserved. Someone once sent me a picture they had taken of me in a yellow slicker. The wind was blowing. I thought, "Well, who is this battered sea-captain type?" Then I looked again and said, "That's you, you silly twit!" I see pictures of myself and I look portentous. Seer-like.

**You've explained your reasons for your preoccupation with death, but what about your preoccupation with children and their death? In *The Loathsome Couple*, children are brutally murdered. And in many of your other books, children meet untimely deaths. Do you really dislike them as much as readers suspect that you do?**

I've never said I dislike children. I really don't know any children except my cousin's little boy, Kenny. He goes around imitating *Star Wars* all the time, and it's very tiresome. He's everything I was not as a child. I was very precocious. I graduated from the eighth grade when I was eleven and was into the high-school syndrome early. I had a super-sophisticated childhood in the suburbs of Chicago.

**Super-sophisticated? How so?**

Privately sophisticated. We had dinner dances and country-club parties and everybody had girlfriends. We got dressed up. Then I went to this super-sophisticated high school in Chicago.[2] I keep looking at Kenny. Apparently life is different now.

**What impresses you most?**

I don't know. I remember fits of childish euphoria that you get while you're still in college, even after. But I also remember thinking of myself as grown-up, being grown-up. Kenny is still very much a kid. He drags it out, doing . . . what do you call those things you do on your bicycle?

**Wheelies.**

Wheelies. Of course, we never had bicycles like that.

**So back then you had lots of girlfriends. But now the press makes a point of the fact that you have never married. What are your sexual preferences?**

Well, I'm neither one thing nor the other particularly.

**Why not?**

I am fortunate in that I am apparently reasonably undersexed or something. I know people who lead really *outrageous* lives.

I've never said that I was gay and I've never said that I wasn't. A lot of people would say that I wasn't because I never do anything about it. What I'm trying to say is that I am a person before I am anything else. Now people come up to you and say, "I'm a press agent" or "I'm a writer." I never say I am a writer. I never say I am an artist.

**You are a person who happens to do those things?**

I am a person who does those things. —I correspond with a museum curator in New York and he told me he was going to be on a TV program about homosexuals speaking out. I asked him, "Are you doing this reluctantly?" And he said, "Oh, no! I am very much into this." He's very militant.

**You don't approve?**

The curator was quoted as saying that his creative life and his homosexuality were one and the same. All I could think was, "Hogwash, dear, hogwash!" Which is unfair, I suppose, because maybe for him the two are linked.

I realize that homosexuality is a serious problem for anyone who is—but then, of course, heterosexuality is a serious problem for anyone who is, too. And being a man is a serious problem and being a woman is, too. Lots of things are problems.

**Is the sexlessness of your books a product of your asexuality?**

I would say so. Although every now and then someone will say my books are seething with repressed sexuality.

**You don't believe that?**

I don't really know. I don't know what I'm writing about. I never sat down and tried to figure it out. It's not about sex, or at least not obviously, right?

**Sometimes it is about sex. There are those who say that your book *The Curious Sofa* is a pornographic novel; in fact, it's even subtitled "a pornographic work." And it's full of couples having odd sexual encounters.**

But it's not pornographic in the standard sense. It's all in the style.

**Why does it end with a man starting up some mechanical device inside of a sofa? Why is the woman frightened? Why a sofa?**

I have absolutely no idea.

**That book is minimalist and unexpected—a good example of your work. You leave a lot to the imagination.**

Well, no one has any sex organs.

**But you do mention several times that the characters are enormously "well endowed."**

Oh, right. But the girls are all flat-chested and the men in the pictures have their backs to you. You don't see anything. The whole point of *The Curious Sofa* is that it was totally not illustrated! I'd rather die than do pornographic drawings. Oh, God!

**Why?**

It's so boring! I wrote *The Curious Sofa* after I finally managed to get a copy of *The Story of O*, which Edmund Wilson had recommended to me as a really great book. I read it with Edmund's strictures in mind, and I thought, "Oh, Edmund, this is absurd. No one takes pornography seriously."

**Do you think there's a difference between pornography and erotica?**

Yes.

**What is a good example of erotica?**

Well, everyone has his tastes. But . . . *Vanity Fair.*[3] It's not one of my favorite books, God knows. It is, however, much more erotic than a novel where everything is spelled out.

**But since you believe so firmly in leaving so much out of your books, how can you believe that they are about reality? Or, in the past, have you just said that for effect?**

No one ever lets me explain what I mean about the reality of my books! Everyone always thinks, "Isn't that amusing that this is his idea of reality!" What I am most interested in is Japanese and Chinese literature. I have always felt that those writers are much better at describing everyday reality—what life is like day to day. I know that my work does not seem to be about reality, but it *is*! God knows that day-to-day reality is certainly drab to the point of lunacy sometimes. And that means that you *have* to leave an awful lot out. I have a fairly eccentric talent, but I try to tone it down rather than heighten it. Most people, I think, take the opposite approach; if they write a novel about everyday life, it winds up being wildly melodramatic. Classical Japanese literature concerns very much what is left out.

**You use this approach?**

I don't use it consciously. I don't say, "Well, I'm going to leave out this and this." It just works out that way. Sometimes the only way I can work is by trying some private, experimental thing. One of the things that George Balanchine has always said is that you don't put everything that there *is* into any one thing that you do. But you do put in everything that you *know*.

**What do you think of this quote from T. S. Eliot: "Humankind can only bear so much reality"?**

Oh, that is so true! I know that quotation. It's perfectly true. We spend all our lives trying to avoid reality in one way or another. I've always had a rather strong sense of unreality. I feel other people exist in a way that I don't.

**What way is that?**

I always feel that other people's lives are filled with meaning. You look at them on the street and think how *real* their lives must be. Of course, you also know that isn't true.

**But don't people think the same of your life?**

I look like a real person, but underneath I am not real at all. It's just a fake persona. That's why cats are so wonderful. They can't talk. They have these mysterious lives that are only half-connected to you. We have no idea what goes on in their tiny little minds.

**You're also fond of another quote from Patrick White[4] that begins "Many too many alternatives, but no choices . . ."**

Right. It's my favorite sentence.

**Why?**

A situation comes up, and either you do this or that, or maybe a third alternative comes up. But you simply do not *choose*. You never really choose anything. It's all presented to you, and then you have alternatives. You don't choose the subject matter of anything you write. You don't choose the people you fall in love with. When I look back on my furious, ill-considered infatuations for people, they were really all the same person. I think everyone has a certain range of experience that doesn't change. You do the same things over again.

**How does this affect your work?**

I find it impossible to sit down cold and say, I'm going to do a book about such and such. Well, that's not *quite* true. I did sit down and do a book about opera—*The Blue Aspic*. Someone had asked me to do an opera book to go along with *The Gilded Bat*, which is about ballet. I said, "I don't know anything about opera, but I'll give it a whirl." So in that sense, I sat down and concentrated on opera, but the idea of a book on opera is meaningless. The actual idea for the book, what it was to be about, had to come to me. I couldn't sit there and construct it. Once the basic idea had come, I could sit and write the book.

**Let me get this straight. Is choice conscious and alternative unconscious?**

No. —I distrust metaphors, and this is a great simplification, but here goes: It's like a department store. The choice has been made for you—you are in umbrellas. You can pick a black umbrella, or a red one, or a blue one. You can pick one with a different handle. But you cannot buy galoshes. And someone in galoshes cannot buy an umbrella. But they can choose any pair of galoshes they want.

**Do you think you were destined to write and draw?**

Yes. I disagree with the quotation about the saddest words of tongue or pen being what might have been. I don't think anything might have been. What is, is. That's the whole idea. Any other idea is remote, such as, "Oh, if only it had been different, Jeanette and I would be gliding down the Nile on a gondola," or "Harold and I would be in Antarctica together," or "I would be a famous movie star." All of this is absolute nonsense. What is, is, and what might have been could never have existed.

**Are you a religious man?**

No.

**But you were raised a Catholic.**

My father's family was Catholic. I skipped first grade and went to a Catholic school for second grade, but the year of my First Communion, I came down with measles or chicken pox or something like that and went to Florida to live with my grandparents for the next year.[5] Somehow or another, I never got back to Catholicism. I don't think I was stuck with it long enough to have one of those terrible love/hate relationships with it. I know a lot of people who have never quite gotten over being Catholic. I do have an aunt who is a nun, but I've never been bothered by that.

**Do you consider yourself a celebrity? Do people recognize you in the street?**

Heavens, no. I'm not a celebrity. People do recognize me, but it is a very minor thing. After *Dracula,* I appeared in *Us* and *People,* so I was beginning to be recognized a lot more. I was also making a lot more money. And I began to realize what it would be like to be rich and famous, but I've decided unh-unh.

**You don't want to be rich and famous?**

I think it would be worse. More of the same and worse.

**You are happy with your cult following?**

Well—no. It's flattering, but it has nothing to do with anything.

**Do you, then, just write for Edward Gorey?**

I know I've said this, but while I realize there is an audience out there, I don't cater to it. I might cater to it if I could figure out how. I've never been particularly goal oriented. If someone would ask me, "How would you summarize your career?" I'd say, "What career?" Or "How would you summarize your work?" and I would say, "What work? Today I am drawing a picture of this and tomorrow I am writing that."

I have a lot of friends in New York who are involved in various enterprises where they're always fanning their careers. They will say, "Listen, I think your next book should be about such and such." I say, "Oh, come now. *What* are you talking about?"

**But you fan your career in a way. You're talking to us, for example, and you're quoted as saying that you only give interviews "on pain of death," yet you give them fairly frequently.**

Yes, but I'm not interested in myself much. And I'm not that interested in my work, except when I'm doing it, which does not make for spectacular entertainment. When I used to finish a project or book, I'd think, "Isn't this wonderful?" And I'd like it for about twenty-four hours. For twenty-four hours, I'd think, "This is the best thing I've done. Isn't this divine? I'm a genius. Whoopee!"

Now that feeling doesn't last thirty seconds. I think, "Well, it's done." I get a certain amount of enjoyment out of doing it; but after it's done, I have no feeling for it at all.

**You said this may be your last interview?**

Yes.

**So what would you like to let people know?**

I can't think of anything else.

**Is there anything people don't understand about you?**

Yes. No. Yes. No. I think I have to leave it up to them. But I'd prefer not to disappear completely, I *would* like to be read.

# The Poison Penman

Richard Dyer,

*The Boston Globe Magazine*, April 1, 1984

"For some reason," says Edward Gorey, "my mission in life is to make everybody as uneasy as possible. I think we should *all* be as uneasy as possible, because that's what the world is like."

These days, Gorey lives in his cousins' vacation home in Barnstable, on Cape Cod, most of the year. It is a quite ordinary-looking house, with painted floors, hooked rugs, summery furniture, a television set, piles of books, three resident cats, and New York City Ballet bath towels (after a design by Gorey). There is only one disquieting detail. On a windowsill lie a number of beanbag birds Gorey has sewn. "I was trying to make penguins, and this is what came out," he explains regretfully. "They look depressed, don't they? There's no way of making them look comfortable." It's no wonder. All of them have broken necks.

At fifty-nine, Gorey looks a little like Alec Guinness, gotten up in a flowing white beard to play some Shakespearean clown licensed to fool the truth. When Gorey goes out, he wears a coyote coat over his jeans and sneakers. Thus dressed, he looks like most of the men in his drawings—or they look like him.

Unfurred, Gorey stretches out on the couch for a long afternoon's chat. Cats nestle in his interstices, although they sometimes jump when he gets excited and waves his heavily ringed hands. His conversation ranges widely over cultural and mass-cultural topics, and he clearly prefers speaking about these to discussing his life and his books. Why concentrate on Edward Gorey, when there is Eve Arden[1] to think about. The personality is playful, amusing, evasive. It's not surprising that he appears in some of his books behind anagrammatic disguises like Regera Dowdy, Dreary Wodge, G. E. Deadworry, Ogdred Weary, and Miss D. Awdrey-Gore.[2]

As Gorey talks, his voice soars and swoops enthusiastically across octaves, and his language takes on the high-flown rhetoric of a Victorian heroine or villain—or of some hapless Edward Gorey protagonist. But he constantly brings his flights back down to earth in the homey idioms of his Midwestern upbringing: "Kiddo," he calls himself; "Heavens to Betsy!" he cries; "Snuggy-poos, *cut it out*," he says to the cats. Gorey's mind is so fertile that his sentences begin and rebegin in a torrent of multiple possibilities. By the end, on the other hand, they tend to trail off inconclusively. Uncertainty and the fragility of every form of order are the subjects that underlie everything.

"What obsesses me more than anything in this world," he says, "is why some things happen and why other things don't. It doesn't seem to me there is any logic, any way of . . . you know . . ."

An only child, Gorey was born in 1925 in Chicago. When he speaks about his childhood, it sounds unusual but not unhappy. "One of the great deprivations of my life is that I never learned how to make papier-mâché, and now it's too late. And everyone else was always making three-dimensional relief maps out of flour and water, and I was never taught to do that."

Gorey's parents, Edward Gorey and Helen Garvey, were divorced when he was eleven and remarried when he was twenty-seven. His stepmother, for a while, was Corinna Mura, a nightclub singer who won a kind of immortality by singing "*La Marseillaise*" in the movie *Casablanca*. Gorey started drawing when he was only one and a half, and his mother preserved these first efforts. "Most children draw a lot, and maybe I drew more than most. We lived in a house on a bluff, and we could watch the trains go by. I drew them, and they look like irregular sausages with windows and wheels. By now I've been drawing for over fifty-five years, and you'd think I might have learned a little bit, but I haven't . . . particularly."

Gorey was a bright kid who skipped grades and spent most of his time reading, playing Monopoly ("It came out when I was about ten, and for months we didn't do anything else"), and going to the movies. He says he was obsessed by serials and horror films, and by whole genres of books. "I loved *The Secret Garden* and the A. A. Milne books. One awful summer my parents sent me to camp, and I spent all my time on the porch reading the Rover Boys. I still reread them now and again. If I liked a book as a child, I assume I would still like it. Both my parents were mystery-story addicts, and I read thousands of them myself. Agatha Christie is still my favorite author in all the world." (One of Gorey's most delightful books, *The Awdrey-Gore Legacy*, is dedicated to Christie.)

The Army interfered with Gorey's plans to attend Harvard. Between 1944 and 1946, Gorey found himself filing morning reports as a company clerk at the Dugway Proving Ground in Utah, the site, he will tell you, where many years later 12,000 sheep were found mysteriously dead. "It was a ghastly place, with the desert looming in every direction, so we kept ourselves sloshed on tequila, which wasn't rationed. The only thing the Army did for me was delay my going to college until I was twenty-one, and that I am grateful for. Not that I got much out of Harvard . . ."

At Harvard, Gorey majored in French, but he says the courses he took were "dim proceedings" during which he "went to sleep after lunch . . . I bounced from the Dean's List to probation and back again." But he did move in significant circles. His Cambridge friends and acquaintances included a number of writers and poets who later became famous: Adrienne Rich, Alison Lurie, John Hawkes, George Plimpton, Donald Hall, John Ashbery, Robert Bly, Kenneth Koch,[3] and Frank O'Hara,[4] who was Gorey's roommate for two years.

Edward Gorey in New York in the early 1950s

"We all sort of gravitated together," Gorey says. "Most of us took John Ciardi's courses in creative writing. I wrote short stories and long poems in unrhymed tetrameter. All of us were *obsessed*. Obsessed by what? Ourselves, I expect."

In a 1975 tribute to O'Hara, Ciardi recalled undergraduates Gorey, O'Hara, and a classmate steaming the "weird wallpaper" from the walls of Ciardi's attic apartment in Medford. "They were at it for days as they played a game of killing insults. They were beautiful and bright and I have never come on three students as a group who seemed to have such unlimited prospects."

Gorey's relationship with O'Hara, who died in an accident on Fire Island in 1966, was close for only that short time at Harvard. In later years, they seldom saw each other. "I have a very vivid impression of him still, but it is nothing that I could put into words," Gorey says. "I knew Frank as a caterpillar before he turned into a butterfly, though he was well on his way by the time we parted company. I was astonished after his death, and even before, when he became a kind of icon for a whole generation. If you know anybody really well, you can never really believe how talented they are. I *know* how he wrote some of those poems, so I can't take them all that seriously. If Rimbaud did it all that long ago, why do it now? I was surprised that Frank lived as long as he did. Every time I saw him, disaster loomed around the corner. For him, it was practically a tenet of belief that nothing has any consequences."

With O'Hara, Gorey went to see Martha Graham dance and to hear premieres of music by Arnold Schoenberg. They checked records of early music out of the Eliot House Library. Gorey hung out at the Mandrake Book Store, then on Mt. Auburn Street. It was there that he had the first exhibition of his pen-and-colored-ink drawings. "Fortunately most of them have disappeared from the face of the Earth, though they were technically more accomplished than what I have been able to do for many years. I once took a Saturday course at the Chicago Art Institute, but that was all the training I had. Sometimes I wonder if I should go off and take life classes and learn to draw, but it's probably too late. I worry that if I did that, whatever I have would probably disappear."

Gorey was also caught up in the activities of the Poets' Theater, which in the early 1950s concentrated the aesthetic energy of the area and the era in a way not seen again until the advent of Peter Sellars at the Boston Shakespeare Company. In that heady art- and self-infatuated atmosphere, Gorey drew posters, designed sets, wrote, and directed a little. "It was the most fun I had in the early days because of the variety of people who were involved—faculty, faculty children, graduates, undergraduates, and strange people."

One of the strangest, the poet V. R. (Bunny) Lang, a great Boston eccentric and *monstre sacré*, became a particularly close friend. The novelist Alison Lurie has left a wonderful, privately published memoir of Lang, who died of Hodgkin's disease in 1956. The cover design is an early graveyard drawing by Edward Gorey.

Gorey's memories of Lang are extensive, funny, poignant, and fresh in his mind even today. "Bunny was extremely talented, but she was one of those people who put as much into her life as she did into her work. She was a fairly large girl with dyed blond hair and her clothes were quite indescribable—she could look rattier than anybody in the history of the world. Yet one night she showed up for supper in Copley Square wearing red fishnet stockings. It was *weeks* before she admitted that she had gotten a job in the chorus line of the Old Howard.[5]

"Night after night in her huge, old-fashioned kitchen on Bay State Road, she would boil down tons and tons of suet, leaving an unbelievable smell. She was trying to manufacture cosmetics. Another job she had was selling baby pictures to new mothers. I used to drive around

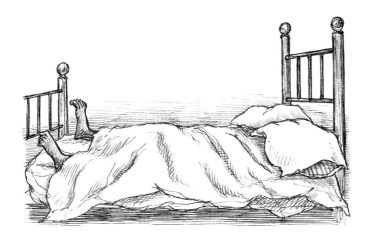

There was a young man, name of Fred,
Who spent every Thursday in bed;
He lay with his feet
Outside of the sheet,
And the pillows on top of his head.

with her to some of the more depressed suburbs of Boston with her blouse buttoned wrongly and her slip hanging out. She said there was no point in approaching a potential customer in a new hat and gloves when the baby had just peed—she wanted the new mother to feel sorry for *her*.

"My last connection with the Poets' Theater was Bunny's play about Orpheus and Eurydice called *Fire Exit*. She was so erratic that everyone went absolutely crackers, but then she could turn around and give a breathtaking performance no professional actress could ever achieve. She was dying, but she kept it a deep dark secret. We went and saw *Waiting for Godot* together just two weeks before she died."

After graduation from Harvard in 1950, Gorey hung around Boston for two and a half years, working part-time in a bookstore, thinking vaguely of getting some kind of job in publishing, and writing the limericks that would become the text for his second book, *The Listing Attic*. At Christmas in 1952, he visited New York, and friends who were at Doubleday found Gorey a job in the design department.

"Doubleday was a pleasant place to work, though I didn't have any great respect for it. I was fast and competent at what I was doing, as opposed to some people in the editorial department, who were scatterbrained to the point of lunacy, so I wrote a lot of my own books at Doubleday. I began with *The Unstrung Harp*, which I thought was a neat trick. I had never written a book before, and it was all about writing, which I didn't know anything about."

Several publishers picked up Gorey's work and then abandoned him. He kept up a steady working pace, varying his own work with illustrations for a number of other books. (He is particularly happy with come contemporary cocktail-party drawings he did for a book called *The Son of Martini Cookbook*.) His best-selling book, *The Curious Sofa*, came in 1961. It is subtitled "A pornographic work," though in fact it leaves everything to the imagination ("Still later Gerald did a terrible thing to Elsie with a saucepan"). *The Hapless Child*, which is dedicated to Bunny Lang, tells the story of the orphaned Charlotte Sophia, punished by teachers for things she didn't do, sold off to a drunken brute, and put to work making artificial flowers, before she is crushed under the wheels of a car driven by her father, who had erroneously been reported killed in a native uprising.

Since the beginning of his New York career, Gorey has spent at least several months a year in a book-cluttered apartment on 38th Street at Madison Avenue that he still maintains. He says there have been "emotional entanglements" in his life, "but I don't wish to get into them. I'm always interested to hear about it when somebody I know gets involved in some totally bizarre relationship, but I know perfectly well I wouldn't want to do it. It's hard enough to sit down to work every day, God knows, even if you are not emotionally involved. Whole stretches of your life go kerplunk when that happens. Sometimes I ask myself why I never ended up with somebody for the rest of my life, and then I realize that I obviously didn't want to, or I would have. I read books about crazed mass murderers, and say to myself, 'There but for the grace of God . . .' Well, not really. All I'd like to do is bop some people over the head. In one way I've never related to people or understood why they behave the way they do. Understand me; I think life is the pits, but I've been very fortunate. I don't have responsibilities to anybody except myself and I have done pretty much what I wanted to do. Fortunately I have never been into drink, drugs, and depravity. I've worked reasonably hard—though not as hard as I should have. I'd love to believe in the possibility of millions and millions of alternative universes. . . ."

Gorey visited Cape Cod for the first time in the summer of 1948 and realized he wanted to live there. Since 1963 he has spent at least half the year in the house in Barnstable. "In New York, the trouble is, if I get out the door, it is fatal; the day is gone. Here, if I get out the door, I get right back in. I have no social life down here at all, except in the summer, when all my relatives are here, and I do the cooking. I can cook almost anything, however complicated, so long as it doesn't have to look pretty when it's over with."

It is clear that Gorey feels a special relationship with oceanside landscapes. He has traveled to Europe only once and amazingly enough has never visited the England that is the setting of nearly all his drawings. His trip was to the Scottish islands, the Shetlands, the Hebrides, and the Orkneys.[6] "I'm not particularly interested in places from a cultural point of view. I went for the scenery rather than anything else. I saw the movie *I Know Where I'm Going*, with Wendy Hiller, and fell in love with the scenery and knew I wanted to go there."

It was in the winter of 1952–1953 that Gorey did inaugurate one of the most important relationships of his life—with the New York City Ballet. "The first year I went to the ballet four or five times, if that. I felt that Balanchine merely illustrated music, and that if you had seen his ballets once, you had seen them. But before long I was attending more often. By 1956 I was going to every performance because it was too much trouble to figure out which twenty-five out of thirty I really had to see. In those days it cost $1.80 to sit in the balcony at the City Center, but we always moved down and sat on the stairs in the front part of the balcony."

Gorey's perfect attendance record at the NYCB continued for twenty-three seasons, until 1979, when he realized that his life would not end if he missed a performance. What he found he was *really* missing was fall on Cape Cod. In recent years Gorey has continued to attend the ballet regularly, though with increasing disappointment and irritation during the decline of balletmaster Balanchine's health and the grooming of Peter Martins as his successor.

I sometimes think if I see that lavender leotard with the little skirt that doesn't quite match in one more ballet...

Two of Gorey's best books, *The Gilded Bat* and *The Lavender Leotard*, are about ballet, and the iconography of ballet appears in many of the others. When he answers the phone in Barnstable, it is often to talk with somebody about the previous night's performance at the NYCB or about what Twyla Tharp is up to. Ballet is one of the many subjects Gorey can talk about indefatigably, dispensing scorn on the critics ("Poor girl," he says of one, "she knows everything about who danced *Giselle* in 1903 but she doesn't have the vaguest idea of what she's seeing right in front of her face") and praising his favorite ballerinas, who include Allegra Kent, Patricia McBride, Maria Calegari, and especially Diana Adams, to whom he dedicated *The Gilded Bat*.

Gorey is entirely and amusingly aware of the way balletomane conversations probably sound to outsiders. Several years ago he did a ballet lobby drawing and text for *Dance Magazine*. The fans are chattering: "She's got a zilch *bourrée*." "His head somehow simply does not read." "She appears to be drying her nail varnish." But Gorey himself is unapologetic about thinking constantly about questions of art. "My life has been concerned completely with aesthetics," he says. "My responses to things are almost completely aesthetic. That means I am always trying to sort of . . . not exactly criticize or analyze. Well, in a sense, you don't just let it wash over you—you translate it into comparisons, into forms of order."

Gorey doesn't particularly like the *Amphigorey* anthologies because "the originals were carefully designed as small books." Part of the fun is not knowing what you are going to find when you turn the page—and when you open an *Amphigorey*, you see four pages at once. The dedications, too, are missing, and they often say something important about the books. Gorey dedicated *The West Wing*, for example, to Edmund Wilson, because the great literary critic was always complaining about the "lameness" of Gorey's writing; this was the first of his books without text. He dedicated *The Willowdale Handcar* to Lillian Gish, because he patterned the amiably peripatetic story after the D. W. Griffith two-reelers she starred in. He dedicated *The Lost Lions* to Gardner McKay, because the story is about something that happened to the leading man on television's *Adventures in Paradise*. Gorey dedicated one book, *The Abandoned Sock*, to a brand of soap. "Who could resist a name like Velveola Souveraine?"

While Gorey is reserved about his best-known accomplishments, his enthusiasm for one conspicuous failure is complete. In 1978, a theatrical adaptation of his work called *Gorey Stories* opened and closed on Broadway in one night. "It was the only time I appreciated my own work, because it had nothing to do with me—somebody else did it. It was first devised at the University of Kentucky and then brought Off-Broadway.[7] I went down and saw it, and the minute I heard things I'd written coming out of other people's mouths, I absolutely adored it, and I went to every performance. In the later previews for Broadway, I thought it was the best ensemble acting I had ever seen in my life. The producers panicked, and the *New York Times* was on strike, so nobody really ever heard about it. But it has gone on and developed a kind of half-life on the amateur circuit, and I hope it will come back again."

This experience didn't satisfy Gorey's longings for practical involvement in movies, ballet, or the theater. Various attempts to prepare ballet scenarios never got anywhere, though he did design the second act of *Giselle* for the transvestite Ballets Trockadero de Monte Carlo.[8] He would still like to write a long-running mystery comedy for the stage. "But the fact is, if I had been in the theater, I would have gone *bonkers* by now because of the endless sitting around. I also don't see myself spending all my time buttering other people up."

In the meantime, there are books to write and illustrate. "There was one delirious period between 1954 and 1957 when I couldn't find a publisher but kept writing, so I actually had a backlog of finished books.

When I started I worried about what would happen if I dried up. W. H. Auden once said that if you are actually working on a poem, you are a poet; the minute you finish you may never write another. By now I must have fifty manuscripts crying out to be illustrated before palsy sets in. I would give my soul to have a finished book at this point. That cardboard box over there—that's full of scribblings of this, that, and the other thing that I'll never get around to doing. I keep having ideas, and I say to myself, 'You'd better get it done, kiddo. Work, for the night is coming.' "

Gorey is even more diffident in talking about his work than he is in talking about himself. "The trouble with interviews is that you say the same things so often you end up believing them."

He will say, "There is almost no heartless work around, so I feel I am filling a small but necessary gap," but then he will immediately tell you he doesn't really mean it. Finally he will say, "I *hate* being characterized. I don't like to read about the 'Gorey details' and that kind of thing. I admire work that is neither one thing nor the other, really. All the things you can talk about in anyone's work are the things that are least important. It's like the ballet. You can describe the externals of a performance—everything, in fact, but what really constituted its core. Explaining something makes it go away, so to speak; what's important is left after you have explained everything else. Ideally, if anything were any good, it would be indescribable. What's the core of Mozart or of Balanchine? That's why I think Henry James is non-existent. The longer he goes on, the more he explains, until there is nothing left."

But in fact, whatever Gorey is talking about is a way of talking about his work, because nearly all his diverse experiences and interests feed into his books. The texts usually come first.

The tone of Gorey's writing owes something to the Edwardian novelist Ronald Firbank.[9] "I'm reluctant to admit that, because I've outgrown him in one way, though in another I don't suppose I ever will. Firbank's subject matter isn't very congenial to me—the ecclesiastical frou-frou, the adolescent sexual innuendo. But the way he wrote things, the very elliptical structure, influenced me a great deal. Frank O'Hara was the only person I've ever known who was able to follow the plots of Firbank, but it never bothered me that I didn't seem to know what was going on."

The texture of Gorey's writing comes out of his comprehensive reading of all the standard and arcane nineteenth-century fiction and, of course, all those mystery stories. And the subject matter comes from all over the place. "Sometimes from the movies or a book, or from something that has actually happened to someone I know. A friend of mine recently told me a dream she had as a child: She went out and got into the family car and went for a drive, and when she came back, the house was gone. I immediately jotted that down, and someday I will do something with it." *The Loathsome Couple* was based on the notorious Moors Murder case in England. "That disturbed me dreadfully, even after years of reading crime stories. I'm all for elegant, cool, goofy murder. This upset me, and it became the one text I felt compelled to write."

Gorey makes all his drawings in an attic studio in the Barnstable house. "I think my drawing is not terribly good at best, but I do know how to illustrate a book better than most. Illustrations shouldn't be smaller than the book—that's why you couldn't possibly illustrate Jane Austen. At the same time, they shouldn't be larger. Aubrey Beardsley's drawings for *Salome* make Oscar Wilde seem in a way rather idiotic. The drawings are so powerful they create their own world, and one more interesting than Mr. Wilde's. They are a perfectly terrible job of illustration, demolishing the text they are attached to."

Gorey speaks with great respect of the work of the great illustrators of the past—of Gustave Doré ("One's entire life would have been settled if one had seen them earlier"), of Sir John Tenniel's illustrations for *Alice in Wonderland*, of Ernest Shepard's illustrations for *The Wind in the Willows*[10] ("the only thinkable ones").

Of his own drawings he says, "I try not to have preconceived ideas so I will not have disappointments. Usually after I have one or two drawings for a book, I have a sense of whether I've made a false start, if I've begun something I can't carry out adequately, or if I can think of something better. My work keeps changing, but I don't think it has progressed in any way, from complicated to simple, or vice versa. But who wants to repeat what they've already done, at least consciously? The Victorian and Edwardian aspect comes, I think, from all those nineteenth-century novels I've read and from nineteenth-century wood engraving and illustration—all that has taken on a strange overtone that it didn't have in those days. Also, because I am not dealing with surface reality, I find the clothes, the decor, and everything of that period more visual. Ultimately it became a kind of habit. I get nervous if I have to do anything contemporary.

"You know, when I look over my books, I am constantly amazed at how little there is in them. Everybody seems to remember much more than there ever actually is, though I don't believe it when people say that everything is between the lines. . . ."

Certain images do recur again and again in Gorey's books: cats, sneakers, fur coats, umbrellas, bicycles, funerary urns shaped like turnips. There is an urn even in his first book, *The Unstrung Harp*. Thirty years later, Gorey published a whole book of them, called *Les Urnes Utiles*. There are urns for croquet balls, for *cartes de visite*, for suet, for vapours, for knobs, for lint (a severed arm lies on the floor behind it). What Gorey characteristic would he put onto or into his own urn?

"I've never really thought about it. But two of my expressions spring to mind: 'Oh, the of it all' and 'Not really.' That's right 'Oh, the of it all' without anything in the middle; just leave the middle out. And, yes, I think, 'Not really.'"

As he says it, he has it both ways, of course. In the question there is the cynic's sigh, and the amusement of an astonished child.

# An American Original

Carol Stevens,

*Print,* January/February 1988

Clavius Frederick Earbrass, the hero of Edward Gorey's first book, *The Unstrung Harp*, is the embodiment of the solitary, eccentric author. Earbrass chooses his titles (before developing a plot) from a list kept in a little green notebook. He wanders aimlessly through what appears to be a somber, late 19th-century mansion, brooding over unwritten sentences. His intimate involvement with his characters, who intrude upon even his most private moments, precludes his intimate involvement with anybody else. For several days after finishing his novel, he remains trancelike in pajamas and robe. Eventually, he reluctantly attends an authors' dinner party, where "the talk deals with disappointing sales, inadequate royalties, idiotic or criminal reviews, and the unspeakable horror of literary life."

Snow was falling when Mr Earbrass woke, which suggested he open *TUH* with the first flakes of what could be developed into a prolonged and powerfully purple blizzard. On paper, if not outdoors, they have kept coming down all afternoon, over and over again, in all possible ways; and only now, at night-fall, have done so satisfactorily. For writing Mr Earbrass affects an athletic sweater of forgotten origin and unknown significance; it is always worn hindside-to.

Gorey at first denies that Earbrass is in any way autobiographical. After some thought, however, he observes, "I've always found it peculiar that the first book I wrote was about an author, because I wasn't an author and I really knew nothing about it. I made the whole thing up and, of course, it's all come true." He further admits to "keeping more notebooks than you'd think humanly possible—of titles, of everything"—and to a previous, but now outgrown, tendency to wander about aimlessly after finishing a manuscript. He would hardly seem to have the time. He has published over fifty books and there are seventy-five more in manuscript form, waiting to be illustrated.

While Gorey bears no physical resemblance to Earbrass, he does resemble several of his other characters, notably the Baron de Zabrus in

Several weeks later, the loofah trickling on his knees, Mr Earbrass mulls over an awkward retrospective bit that ought to go in Chapter II. But where? Even the voice of the omniscient author can hardly afford to interject a seemingly pointless anecdote concerning Ladderback in Tibet when the other characters are feverishly engaged in wondering whether to have the pond at Disshiver Cottage dragged or not.

*The Gilded Bat* (though Gorey has grey hair and a friendlier demeanor); Emblus Fingby in *The Osbick Bird*; and perhaps most of all, the author in *The Chinese Obelisks* who goes for a walk attired in white Keds and a voluminous fur coat, staples of Gorey's own wardrobe. Unlike these three figures, however, whose hair grows low on their foreheads and who, from the side, appear to have had their heads affixed to their necks horizontally, on the long side of the oval, Gorey has a high, balding forehead and an imposing presence, and even bareheaded seems as tall as the Baron in his top hat. He further embellishes his already eccentric appearance by wearing an impressive collection of antique rings, which he has been known to twist off into an ashtray before going to work at the drawing board. Behind this flamboyant exterior, however, is a shy, amiable man who answers his own phone, is reluctant to let anyone down by refusing an assignment (even though it occasionally might be in his best interest to do so), and isn't at all sinister.

It may have been Dracula who originally set Gorey on his horror-strewn path. An only child, Gorey is reported to have taught himself to read at three and a half. Two years later, he discovered both *Dracula* and *Alice in Wonderland*, which left him with an enduring fondness for Victorian novels and 19th-century illustration. When he wasn't reading, he was drawing. "Many kids do," he observes. "I just kept at it longer." He attended Francis W. Parker, a private, progressive school where he remembers "a very good art teacher," and studied at the Art Institute on Saturdays. Mostly, he is self-taught. When he was eleven years old, his parents divorced in circumstances which themselves have a Victorian ring. When Gorey was twenty-seven, they remarried each other.

[After graduating from Harvard], through his friendship with Jason Epstein, founding editor of Doubleday's line of literary and scholarly paperbacks, Anchor Books, Gorey came to New York in 1953 and on the strength of a portfolio of fake bookjackets, which, he says, were "as uncommercial as you can reasonably get," was hired as a staff artist. "He was on the drawing boards," recalls art director Diana Klemin, "fixing mechanicals [for freelancers like Leonard Baskin and Ben Shahn][1], doing paste-ups and designing jackets. He was just right for Anchor Books, especially for Proust and Conrad." It is amusing to picture Gorey in the staid corporate world of the 1950s, sweeping through the halls in his fur coats, wearing jeans and a beard when it wasn't at all fashionable, and decorating his corner of the office with skeletons, puppets, and little pieces of sculpture.

Somehow, he found time to write and illustrate his own books, the first four of which (*The Unstrung Harp*, *The Listing Attic*, *The Doubtful Guest*, and *The Object-Lesson*) had been published by the time Gorey left Doubleday in 1960 to join Jason Epstein and Norman Podhoretz at The Looking Glass Library, where he served as editor and art director. After a subsequent uncongenial stint as art director of Bobbs Merrill, a position from which he was mercifully fired after a year, he discovered he had so much freelance work that he didn't have time to look for another job. "I never had the guts to say purposefully, 'OK, I'm quitting my job, I'm freelancing,'" he observes. "And it was years before I realized that was what I was actually doing." Not being on anybody's staff gave him the freedom to spend most of his time on Cape Cod, coming to New York only to indulge his passion for the dance. During the season, he attended every performance of the New York City Ballet and often found time to take in Paul Taylor and Twyla Tharp as well.

Gorey's characters, more often than not, assume Balanchine poses. They are depicted in a kind of cinematic perspective, as if each drawing were a framed still, against a scrupulously detailed, tightly cross-hatched background. Gorey admits to conflicting feelings about this labor-intensive rendering.

In an effort to avoid what he calls "cross-hatching as a way of life," he sometimes adopts a looser style or, at the very least, sets his figures against a white background. Describing an alternate, sketchy version of *The Chinese Obelisks*, which he published in the second anthology of his work, *Amphigorey Also*, Gorey says, "I have a fondness for these drawings because I seldom do that kind of thing." They are, however, close in feeling to the rough thumbnail doodles that serve, along with pages listing nonsense words and their variations, as preliminary outlines for his stories. He says he is sometimes inspired by a visual image, sometimes by a line of poetry, and sometimes by the beginning of a plot. He works in pen-and-ink or watercolor, on Strathmore two-ply medium-finish, except when the weather on the Cape is too damp for him to draw at all.

These days, Gorey has a devoted, enthusiastic, and still-growing following, but he began slowly. The initial sales of his first four books came to only about 1500 each and he didn't stay with any one publisher very long. Sometimes he produced his books himself under the Fantod Press imprint. ("Fantod" is an obscure word, usually used in the plural, meaning willies or fidgets.)

Andreas Brown, proprietor of the Gotham Book Mart, a Manhattan bookstore specializing in poetry, literature, theater, and art books that are both in and out of print and not available at more commercially oriented outlets, feels that Gorey's work must be handled with personal attention. Originally motivated to collect and promote Gorey's work because he liked it so much himself and believed in Gorey's genius, Brown has found that specializing in something that isn't readily available elsewhere to Gorey's followers is profitable. Gorey remarks cheerfully that Brown has turned him into a "cottage industry," showing his work in the Gotham Gallery; selling, besides his books, his T-shirts and greeting cards; and conceiving the notion for a large-sized anthology of the small editions that are no longer in print, an idea that resulted in the publication of *Amphigorey*, *Amphigorey Too*, and *Amphigorey Also*.

While Gorey's work has gained in popularity by virtue of its own intrinsic fascination, Brown's enthusiastic marketing, and perhaps as a result of a kind of natural momentum, there was also *Dracula*. In 1973, John Wulp, a theatrical producer, writer, and designer who is now director of the Playwrights' Horizons Theater School in New York,[2] decided to stage a summer theater production of *Dracula* on Nantucket. On the casual suggestion of an old friend at a cocktail party, he telephoned Gorey, whom he had never met, and asked him to design the sets and costumes. Gorey, whose interest in theater stemmed from his own playwriting days at Harvard and his involvement with the Poets' Theater, replied, with customary amiability, "Sure, why not?" His black-and-white sets were heavily cross-hatched and bookish, emphasizing the literary origins and time period of the original work, but the illustrative quality and flat perspective also served to convey an objective, contemporary satirical point of view. The production was so successful that Wulp decided to take it to Broadway.

Gorey, who felt that "what looks swell on the page of a book in black-and-white cross-hatching does not necessarily look great on the stage," wanted to re-do the production in, according to Wulp, "mushroom-like colors." "But I learned one of the first lessons of the theater," Gorey recalls. "If it works, don't change it." He dutifully added space and detail to his original designs, rendering his illustrations at one quarter inch to a foot instead of the standard one half inch to avoid "acres of cross-hatching," and gratefully delivered them to scenic supervisor Lynn Pecktal, who built models, drew plans, and shepherded the production through two different scenic-building and painting studios.

Although Gorey professes to have no talent for designing in three dimensions, some of the best of *Dracula*'s concepts were his: the cav-

ernous vaulted space into which three separate scenes—a library, a bedroom and a crypt—could be introduced, the characteristically Gorey bat
ornamentation, the solitary vivid-red accent (at director Dennis Rosa's
behest, the splash of red found its way into each act—as a glass of wine,
a rose, and a drop of blood), and the wittily sinister Gothic atmosphere.
In fact, though Gorey neither wrote, produced, nor directed the show, it
was always referred to as "The Edward Gorey production of *Dracula*."

Theatrical productions are generally the result of an intensely collab-
orative process. That *Dracula* was so indisputably Gorey's says a great
deal about his way of working. "Collaborating with Edward is not collaboration," says Wulp. "You don't have a discussion about concept or
anything like that. He meets once with the director, evolves a ground
plan for the entrances and exits, and then goes home and does his

designs. Even then, there's never an overall drawing of what it's going to look like. He does elevations section by section and mails them to you." What collaboration exists is a kind of reverse process. Pecktal would say, "We need a twenty-five-foot by twenty-five-foot backdrop to go off behind the terrace doors"—and Gorey would readily oblige.

Wulp has worked with Gorey on a number of productions since the original Nantucket *Dracula*, including *Swan Lake*, *Giselle,* and *Le Bal de Madame H.* for the Eglevsky Ballet; *The Mikado*, with the drama department at Carnegie Mellon; and two shows which Gorey wrote and designed: *Gorey Stories* (at the WPA Theater and later on Broadway) and *Tinned Lettuce*, with the undergraduate drama department at New York University.[3] Wulp enjoys being surprised by the Gorey version of whatever it is. "What you need is to be absolutely faithful to Edward," he asserts. "You have to be interested in just letting him do what he wants."

Gorey collaborates best when he is sympathetic to the work in question. "Quite often, I'm surprised when I'm asked to do something," he remarks, "because I would have thought that only I would know that I would like to do it." On the other hand, he is appalled by art directors who entirely misread him. After the publication of his pseudo-pornographic story, The Curious Sofa, in which anything that may or may not happen is supplied by the reader's imagination, Gorey received a number of calls from people who wanted him to illustrate genuinely pornographic novels. "I would blush crimson at the other end of the phone," Gorey recalls. "I couldn't possibly draw anybody of either sex doing anything." Clifford Ross, a longtime fan and friend of Gorey's who, as a senior at Yale in 1974, organized an exhibit of Gorey's work which subsequently traveled to university libraries and small museums throughout the country, observes, "He has a very distinct style, aesthetic, and set of values and the extent to which he's made to compromise those, I think, dilutes the strength of his work. Edward is rather like chamber music. You can't turn him into a symphony."

Although he makes an occasional appearance at New York's annual Book Country street fair to sign books, Gorey for the most part keeps gracefully aloof from efforts to promote his work. His friends and supporters continue to investigate merchandising possibilities, not to commercialize him but to give him the financial security to indulge as yet unconjured Gorey visions. In the meantime, Gorey stays on Cape Cod with his five cats, working on his own books and dutifully supplying drawings for other projects when they are requested. Asked about his future plans, he replies, "I'd love to come up with something really outrageous, but what, these days, would be considered really outrageous?"

# Edward Gorey
# and the Tao of Nonsense

Stephen Schiff,

*The New Yorker*, November 9, 1992

M any of Edward Gorey's most fervent devotees think he's
(a) English and (b) dead. Actually, he has never so much as visited either place. But his work has imprinted itself on the American consciousness as something from long ago and far away. Most of us by now
have seen it somewhere or other—the sets and costumes he designed for
*Dracula* in 1978, the swooning logos for the PBS television series
*Mystery!*, or possibly the hundreds of book covers and newspaper illustrations he has turned out over the last forty years. Less prominent, but
more important, are the small books he has been producing in quantity
since 1953—albums of enchanting pen-and-ink drawings accompanied

Mr Earbrass has received the sketch for the dust-wrapper of *TUH*. Even after staring at it continuously for twenty minutes, he really cannot believe it. Whatever were they thinking of? That drawing. Those colours. *Ugh*. On any book it would be ugly, vulgar, and illegible. On his book it would be these, and also disastrously wrong. Mr Earbrass looks forward to an exhilarating hour of conveying these sentiments to Scuffle and Dustcough.

by carefully hand-lettered texts that are spooky, funny, and, in the end, often quite unnerving. The books are like the remnants of a once proud civilization whose decline and fall have resulted not from dwindling armies or crumbling economies but from an invasion of the inexplicable—random brutality, spates of angst and ennui, odd words and odder weapons, and the kind of skittering beasties you catch only out of the corner of your eye.

Not surprisingly, perhaps, Gorey himself appears to be a migrant from another century. Beneath a baldish head and trifocals he wears a thick cloud of mustache and a white beard in the profuse, flowing style of a grand British litterateur—Trollope, maybe, or Shaw. It's not hard to imagine him sinking into the hungry upholstery of some mahogany-panelled library, snipping a Havana before the roaring fire, and then turning toward the BBC camera to recite, in lugubrious tones, from his own neo-Edwardian prose. But Gorey is in every way a surprise. If you expect orotund pronouncements from beneath that cascading beard, what you get instead is a voice that's high, nasal, and unmistakably campy. "Actually, I find myself more and more glued to the TV set," he says, with a snort of mock exasperation. "I'm passionately devoted to reruns. Like, for instance, up until just last week, late in the afternoon, you could watch three different *Golden Girls* reruns in the space of an hour and a half. I've seen them all fifteen times, I'm sure. And also I'm very partial to certain surrealist sitcoms. There was one called *Stat*, a medical one. It had—oh dear. One of those actors whose name is Ron."

Gorey's conversation is speckled with whoops and giggles and noisy, theatrical sighs. He can sustain a girlish falsetto for a very long time and then dip into a tone of clogged-sinus skepticism that's worthy of Eve Arden. He wears a gold earring in each ear, and there are rings on his fingers—heavy brass and iron ones, arranged in piles. As he talks, he flaps his slender hands, and the rings clank.

We are sitting in the kitchen of his rambling Cape Cod home—"It's the only bearable room in the house"—and when you see him up close, like this, the beard and glasses and oddly severe grey-blue eyes come to seem a kind of old-codger disguise. For, at sixty-seven, Gorey is improbably youthful, his skin unwrinkled and spotless and baby-pink, his sprigs of white hair as fine as a newborn's. He's a lanky man who never sits in a chair when he can flop, and, though his presence is as drastically stylized as his books, he appears to be without pretension. Gorey is opinionated, and even, at times, vicious, but he's almost child-ishly unaware that anyone might find what he says objectionable; one has the impression that if he actually discovered himself giving offense, the remorse would overwhelm him. Listening to the peaks and troughs of his inflections may make you feel as though everyone else on earth were speaking in a monotone, but there is also a danger of not taking him seriously enough: of mistaking him for a standard-issue small-town eccentric who, for his own good, should probably never have been granted cable.

Yet Gorey turns out to be a man of enormous erudition, his intake of television trash merely part of a larger cultural voraciousness. During the thirty years he spent in New York, from 1953 to 1983, he became renowned in certain circles for attending virtually every performance of the New York City Ballet, always wearing the same picturesque getup: the beard, of course, which melted into a floor-length fur coat; blue-jeans and slim white tennis shoes; a long scarf and, often, a necklace or pendant; a variety of massive rings. His appearance was half bongo-drum beatnik, half fin-de siècle dandy. Night after night (and matinée after matinée), Gorey would spend intermissions on a bench at the left side of the New York State Theater's promenade, and a coven of promi-nent balletomanes would gather around him—to "tear their hair out over what they'd just seen," according to one of them, the critic Arlene Croce. Gorey was vociferous in his admiration for City Ballet's great choreographer, George Balanchine, and when Balanchine died in 1983, he took it as his cue to move out of New York entirely—an act of aes-theticism worthy of Oscar Wilde. But Gorey's learning doesn't end with the ballet. He has also read more novels, examined more paintings, lis-tened to more classical music, and seen more movies than many special-ists in those fields. He has roomed with poet Frank O'Hara, has illus-trated Samuel Beckett and T. S. Eliot,[1] and, during his Harvard days, just after the Second World War, he befriended and influenced a throng of future literary stars from Alison Lurie to John Ashbery. He can converse as lucidly on *The Tale of Genji*, the films of Feuillade,[2] and the legato line of the ballerina Diana Adams as on the more elusive charms of *Knots Landing*. None of which would matter very much if he were not himself an artist and writer of genius.

His books have never attracted more than a cult audience, though when they were gathered together in a series of anthologies, they sold modestly well. In New York, a small squadron of Gorey devotees has been trying for several frustrating years to make his name a household word; he seems to tolerate their efforts, but can't bring himself to participate much. "Edward has kept himself protected from success," says his friend Clifford Ross, an artist and producer who has known him for over twenty years. "I was telling him on the phone about some of the projects we were working on for him, but he wasn't responding. Finally he said, 'Oh, I suppose that means now I can die.' Sometimes with him nothing happens, because nothing is exactly what he wants to happen."

Still, a lot is happening at the moment. An evening of musical theater called *Amphigorey*, which has already enjoyed a successful run with Cambridge's American Repertory Theater, is being prepared for a New York opening. It's an adaptation of various Gorey works, published and unpublished, including *The Blue Aspic*, about a psychotic opera fan; *The Admonitory Hippopotamus*, in which a mysterious pachyderm ruins a woman's life by uttering a cryptic phrase over and over in the manner of Poe's raven; and *The Curious Sofa: A Pornographic Work*, which follows a grape-eating demirep named Alice through a series of unspecified encounters with various "well-favored" men, women, and sheepdogs. (It contains the immortal line "Still later Gerald did a terrible thing to Elsie with a saucepan.")

When I ask Gorey how he feels about this spasm of promotion, he thrusts his head back and looses one of his hyperbolic sighs. "It's very sweet if somebody wants to do this," he says. "But you'd better be prepared, because it probably isn't going to happen. Besides, you know, I find it difficult to help out or collaborate, and since I don't want to leave the Cape, or anything, the only way I could collaborate is if someone came up here for a couple of months and sat around."

Sitting around is mostly what he does. Gorey is a confirmed recluse, and really always was, even in the days when he was so obsessively out on the town. "If I'm working very hard, which is very seldom, the last thing I want to do in order to relax is to be with people and babbling away and so forth," he says. "So I go to the movies or read a book or watch any of my thousands of tapes upstairs. Most of my friends in New York were my friends because we were all so busy going to things we had no time to do anything else. I might never have seen people if I didn't see them that way. Social events—*foof*. You know."

I ask if he was ever a partygoer.

"No. I'm slightly deaf—more than slightly. And for years I've had a terrible time at intermissions and things. I just stand there smiling sweetly, and I wonder what everybody's *talking* about because I can't hear one word in ten from the background noise. And also when I talk to people I really like to talk to them, and not just exchange pleasantries and wonder which of us is going to try to get away first. Most social occasions leave me less than enthralled. I mean, you read about these wonderful parties at Lady Ottoline Morrell's[3] and everybody was there and everybody was so brilliant and the conversation was transcendental, and I don't believe this for one minute. There have been winters up here where I saw hardly anyone, and I don't remember feeling particularly bothered by it."

Friends are at a loss to explain the darkness in his work, because they detect none in the man himself. Still, Gorey can be perplexing. He never travels. In fact, he has gone out of the country only once, and then he went to the remote Scottish isles—the Orkneys, the Shetlands, and the Outer Hebrides. Nowadays, even the thought of a trip to New York fills him with dread. He has complained at times of feeling "unreal," and his friend Consuelo Joerns, a writer and artist who has known him since 1938, recalls, "He said to me once that he hates to travel, because when he's between places he's nowhere." Although he's a regular customer at a rustic cafeteria-style restaurant near his home called Jack's Out Back, he admits that he doesn't even visit friends. "It sounds sort of snotty, but I feel that I'm much better off if people come to me than me go to them. We all have periods when we're shining very brightly and people are calling us up and wanting us to do things and so forth, and then somehow the phases of the moon change and we're hardly visible at all and the phone doesn't ring for days. I just go along with that. I wait for the phone to ring, usually."

Gorey refused to attend the New York opening of *Dracula* (he thought the production a bit of a "hodgepodge"); he also refused to attend the Tony-presentation ceremony that year, at which he won the award for best costume design. Is he immune to the lure of fame? "I really don't think I was ever terribly ambitious. And the more I go along, the more I think how awful it would be to be rich and famous. I'd love to be rich, but being famous—I think if you ever give any thought to it, then you say, 'Well, you know, I'm not famous *enough*. Why don't I have a one-man show at the Metropolitan Museum?' And this way you drive yourself absolutely crackers. So I try not to think about it. I occasionally have my fantasies of worldwide fame, you know, but they're totally absurd. More and more, I think you should have no expectations and do everything for its own sake. That way you won't be hit in the head quite so frequently. I firmly believe what someone said—that life is what happens when you're making other plans."

If Gorey seems to be striving to confine himself to the margins of American culture, his books look less marginal all the time—especially in a society increasingly devoted to pastiche and appropriation. "God knows my influences are eclectic," he says. "There's hardly anything I haven't filched some time or another. Silent films, especially serials—I really do believe that movies got worse once they started to talk. Japanese literature, because I think I've read everything that's available in translation until about 1900, and they do have that tradition I love of leaving things out. The big, long nineteenth-century novel with a cast of thousands. And then nineteenth-century book illustration. I was very much taken with that, in the same way that I presume Max Ernst was. I mean, all those things that Ernst used in his collages *can't* have looked that sinister to people in the nineteenth century who were just leafing through ladies' magazines and catalogues. And, of course, now they look nothing but sinister, no matter what. Even the most innocuous Christmas annual is filled with the most lugubrious, sinister engravings."

Gorey's chosen form is a kind of subversive imitation of the children's book; his albums intentionally evoke the remembered comforts of childhood reading. There isn't much text in them, for instance, and what there is is terse and seemingly straightforward. Sometimes it takes the shape of an alphabet; sometimes it rhymes. The drawings have the nostalgic feel of nineteenth-century engravings; their vibrant intensity is reminiscent of Tenniel or Gustave Doré, or even of a Currier & Ives holiday card. And the world they depict is like something out of *The*

*Secret Garden:*[4] vaguely Victorian or Edwardian, and chockablock with swirling wallpaper, jittery carpets, ponderous draperies, tea sets, balustrades, urns. It's a flat, two-dimensional universe, and one of Gorey's central jokes is the game he plays with turn-of-the-century art history, recapitulating the way Cézanne and Matisse disrupted perspective to bring color and pattern to the fore. Except that Gorey's world is usually colorless—and often cross-hatched to the point of mania. Pattern competes with pattern, rugs battle wall panels, and the characters themselves become clashing design elements, featureless bubble-heads floating atop vast swatches of herringbone and fustian and fur. Gorey's people wear things nobody wears anymore—curly waxed mustaches, plus-fours, feathers that erupt from the crowns of their heads. Their faces are sometimes wildly stylized and sometimes not, but they are almost always disturbingly blank.

A Gorey book feels like a whimsy for children, but it doesn't develop that way. Several pages in, or sometimes immediately, ghastly things start happening. Young Millicent Frastley is abducted and sacrificed to The Insect God. Maudie Splaytoe, the prima ballerina known to the public, is lost over the Camargue when "a great dark bird" flies into the propeller of her airplane. Poor Charlotte Sophia, the heroine of *The Hapless Child*, is run over by her own father, who then fails to recognize her. And in Gorey's most celebrated alphabet, *The Gashlycrumb Tinies*, a tyke perishes with every passing letter:

A is for AMY who fell down the stairs
B is for BASIL assaulted by bears . . .
K is for KATE who was struck with an axe
L is for LEO who swallowed some tacks
M is for MAUD who was swept out to sea
N is for NEVILLE who died of ennui . . .

Gorey's horrors are related in a kind of cultivated deadpan, as though the narrator, still enjoying his fireside brandy, hadn't quite grasped the gravity of the situation. Strange creatures, often little newtlike things, appear, undetected, in corners. And the drawings correspond oddly to the words; sometimes they, too, seem oblivious of what's going on. If the reader thought he was embarking on a sugary pipe dream, the scales will by now have fallen from his eyes. Reading Gorey is like losing your innocence—except that, as the creepiness mounts, something else takes over. His victims are too vacuous to inspire pity and terror, and his tone is too cool to make you wring your hands. The only recourse is to laugh, and you do. In some of Gorey's finest stories, a kind of nameless angst descends: you watch a whole life pass by with woefully little inci- dent, or you watch a house invaded by an ineffable presence, almost without repercussion. For Gorey, existential dread isn't the subtext, it's the punch line. The books are as appallingly funny as if they were parody, but they're not parody, exactly, because in some way they also seem absolutely true; their chill is authentic. As Gorey has said, only half in jest, "I write about everyday life."

He hates to think of his work as "macabre," because he never lingers on the violence; in fact, he invests it with no emotion at all. People— often tiny people—are dispatched, and life goes on. (When I ask him why so many of his victims are children, Gorey replies, "It's just so obvi- ous. They're the easiest targets.") In a very beautiful, underrated 1962 book called *The Willowdale Handcar* Gorey offers a subtle yet magisterial view of the human condition, following three of his typical nondescript turn-of-the-century characters on a handcar voyage through America. Along the way, they pass people and places with wonderfully Goreyesque names: Mr. Queevil in Bogus Corners, Nellie Flim some- where between West Elbow and Penetralia, and Mrs. Umlaut, who is mentioned during a baked bean supper at the Halfbath Methodist

*Some months went by, and still they had not returned to Willowdale.*

Church, near Hiccupboro. *The Willowdale Handcar* is a kind of denatured American picaresque; it's like *Huckleberry Finn* or *On the Road* or *They Live by Night*, except that the characters aren't rogues or rebels, they're the usual Gorey ciphers, hurtling through time. Poker-faced, they traverse a landscape that's like something out of D. W. Griffith, and obscure disasters take place around them—some momentarily arresting, some only dimly perceived, all without much consequence. An air of almost metaphysical mystery surrounds this journey, just as it surrounds so many of Gorey's journeys; in the end, the three companions disappear into a tunnel and fail to come out the other side. Gorey's world is the world depicted in Brueghel's great painting *The Fall of Icarus*, in which a plowman and a crew of seamen go about their business while the mythical flier splashes into the sea next to them almost unnoticed. "If anything, I'm a Taoist,"[5] he says. "You know, the Way. Go with the flow. Keep in tune with it all."

Gorey is miserable discussing his work. His eyes dart. Gradually, he withdraws into a silence punctuated by "tsk"s and groans. The darkness, the sadism, the bloodshed—questions about these things disturb him the most. He feels misunderstood. His books aren't in the gothic tradition, he insists; he's not telling horror stories; he's not out to scare. What he's up to has more to do with nonsense, with Lewis Carroll and Edward Lear (whose poems he has spectacularly illustrated). "Nonsense really demands precision," he says. "Like in *The Jumblies*: 'Their heads are green, and their hands are blue. And they went to sea in a sieve.' Which is all quite concrete, goofy as it is." Well, yes. But no fate more dire than a meal of Stilton cheese ever befalls the Jumblies. Contrast that with the phlegmatic Gorey limerick that runs:

> Little Zooks, of whom no one was fond,
> They shot through the roof and beyond;
> The infant's trajectory passed him over the rectory
> And into a lily-choked pond.

Gorey shifts uneasily in his chair. "O.K.," he says. "Well, I think I'm much more optimistic than I am pessimistic. But every now and then I do think life is a crock, there's no getting around it. Basically, it's really just *aw*ful. I do think it's stupidity that makes the world go round. And if you're doing nonsense it *has* to be rather awful, because there'd be no point. I'm trying to think if there's sunny nonsense. Sunny, funny nonsense for children—oh, how boring, boring, boring. As Schubert said, there is no happy music. And that's true, there really isn't. And there's probably no happy nonsense, either."

An orangey-brown cat slinks up Gorey's arm and onto his shoulders, where it stretches for a moment before draping itself athwart him like a stole. "Dear! What are you *doing?*" he says, but he really doesn't seem to mind. Gorey tolerates a wide range of feline behavior—and that is just as well, since he keeps seven cats, only three of which ever appear for company. "The cats abuse him," his old friend Consuelo Joerns says. "The thing that horrifies me is that they'll spill his jar of India ink all over a drawing he's been working on for a week, and he won't do anything, he'll just—Well, he really is a Taoist. He has a tendency to let things be. The only time he ever interferes is when he's rescuing stray cats. And I think he also picks up worms off the sidewalk, so they don't get stepped on."

"Most people who have cats would not put up with what I put up with from my cats," Gorey says, reaching back with one gangly arm to give his purring stole a stroke. "You know—clawed furniture, cats who pee all over the place, and everything. But I feel it's their house as much as mine. What I do like about them is since they don't talk, that's sort of a plus. And they really are very mysterious. It's impossible to know what's going on in their tiny noggins. It's very interesting sharing a house with a group of people who obviously see things, hear things, think about things in a vastly different way."

Gorey has rarely shared a house with anybody else. Since leaving college, in 1950, he has cultivated the life of a vestal, the anchoritic handmaiden of his art, summering with cousins when they visited Cape Cod but otherwise living alone. He has said that he is "reasonably undersexed," a condition for which he seems somewhat grateful, but now I ask him whether he has ever been in love, and his eyes, which are never easy to read, momentarily narrow. "Oh, moot question," he says. "I thought I was in love a couple of times, but I rather think it was only infatuation. It bothered me briefly, but I always got over it. I mean, for a while I'd think, after some perfectly pointless involvement that was far more trouble than it was worth—I'd think, 'Oh God, I hope I don't get infatuated with anybody ever again.' And it's been sixteen, seventeen years, so I think I'm safe. I realized I was accident-prone in that direction anyway, so the hell with it. Cats have the same sort of nuisance value, so to speak. They occupy one."

The house is somewhat redolent of Gorey's companions, but that's the least of its peculiarities. He walks me through it in a rather gingerly fashion, wary of a newcomer's reaction. The place is big—with cavernous rooms—and sits prominently on a typical New England village green. All around it are bright-white houses with acres of buzz-cut lawn. But Gorey's house looks like something out of *Grey Gardens*—the paint reduced to a kind of dandruff, the grounds fully capable of harboring anacondas and rare medicines. Out front sits his morose-looking Volkswagen Rabbit, with the license plate that reads "Ogdred"; it's one of his pseudonyms, almost all of which are anagrams of his name: Ogdred Weary, Dogear Wryde, D. Awdrey-Gore, G. E. Deadworry, Drew Dogyear, and so forth. On the crumbling porch is a bench, but no one can sit on the bench, because it's lined with rocks. There are also rocks, arranged in various Zen ways, in the living room and the front room. Next to the kitchen sink are two bowls full, and these rocks are covered with water, and the water is covered with algae. "Don't worry," he says. "I'm not making them into fettucine or anything. But I do like rocks. I had a terrible trauma this week: I didn't know what had become of my favorite rock. And I thought, Oh my God, I can't live. Fortunately, it was found."

The house was built around 1800, and it's clear that once upon a time, Gorey began to fix it up. There are lots of bookshelves, and a few walls with fairly fresh paint on them; there are fine wood floors, and here and there, if you can catch a glimpse of them, lovely antique tables and mirrors and chests. But almost all the best pieces have long since been buried under thousands of dusty books—mostly the kind you'd find in a secondhand bookstore—and, if not books, then videotapes and CDs and cassettes, and, if not those things, well . . . other things. Finials, for instance. In the vast living room, there are finials of every size and sort—huge free-standing ones and little delicate ones—some on shelves, some just sitting out on the floor. There are lobster floats and other vaguely nautical whatsits stacked against walls and tucked behind looming, cat-clawed sofas. By a fireplace stands a perfect old toilet, and on the floor, half concealed under a table, lies an enormous tusk. The ceiling bears a number of deep wounds, mostly patched with cardboard, and a vine is growing through one of the walls; Gorey says he once determined to go out and cut it down, but he could never find out where it began.

"The house has a somewhat, um, distressed look," I offer.

"Oh, well, yes," he says. "It really does need an awful lot of work, and if I got a large sum of money I would have it all fixed up—though I'm not sure I would have much of the inside fixed up more than it is. I rather like decay. I'm a little reluctant to take out a mortgage. Being free-lance, you never know."

Gorey's is clearly the sensibility of a collector—or maybe "amasser" would be a better word. He wants to buy every book he sees, wants to see every movie that plays (he even goes to sequels of *Friday the 13th* and *Nightmare on Elm Street*), wants to watch every episode of his favorite TV shows. When I ask him what he gets out of all this cultural consumption, he says, "I don't know. It keeps real life at bay, I suppose. Every now and again, I think, 'If I don't go and see this, how will I know?' But then I do go and see it and I already did know, exactly."

"He has a certain kind of addictive personality, and it expresses itself in every way," his friend Charles France, the former American Ballet Theater executive, says. "It's intriguingly compulsive behavior. It's like all that cross-hatching in his drawings. There he goes for thirty years, cross-hatching—he can't stop doing it."

Gorey began drawing, he says, when he was one and a half—"little sausagey things that were supposed to be trains." That was back in Chicago, where he was born, in 1925. His father was a newspaper reporter who later dabbled in politics and publicity; his mother, a beauty, worked as a government clerk. Edward, known then and now as Ted, was an only child and precocious: he taught himself to read at the age of three. "Nobody knows how," he says. "I find it absolutely baffling." He saw very little of his father when he was young, but his mother was of the smothering variety. "We were far closer than I really wished most of the time, and we fought a good deal right up until the time she died, at the age of eighty-six," he says. "She was a very strong-minded lady." Gorey remembers his childhood as happy and normal, but there was one wrenching element. "We moved around a lot—I've never under-stood why. We moved around Rogers Park in Chicago, from one street to another, about every year." By the time he finished the eighth grade (he skipped the first and the fifth), he had attended five different schools.

Then, when he was eleven, his parents divorced (apparently amica-bly; they remarried sixteen years later). Ted went off to the progressive Francis W. Parker high school, and there found himself a star among stars. "He was considered brilliant and funny," says Consuelo Joerns, who dated him in those days. "And there was something futuristic about him. He was two steps ahead of the rest of us. Once, he painted his toenails green and walked barefoot down Michigan Avenue, which was really shocking in those days."

Gorey spent a semester after high school at the Art Institute of Chicago, but in 1943 he was drafted into the Army and assigned to be a company clerk at the Dugway Proving Ground near Salt Lake City. "They tested mortars and poison gas," he says. "Whenever you read that somewhere in the Western states twenty thousand sheep have expired for some mysterious reason, it's always the Dugway Proving Ground." Accepted by Harvard before he was drafted, Gorey enrolled after his discharge and majored in French. His roommate was Frank O'Hara, later the most celebrated poet of the New York School. At an exhibition of Gorey drawings at Cambridge's Mandrake Book Store, O'Hara met the future poet John Ashbery, and soon a gang formed that would eventually include Alison Lurie, Kenneth Koch, Donald Hall, and the poet-actress-playwright who became their den mother and sacred monster—the late V. R. (Bunny) Lang. With Lang and O'Hara (and a host of other poets, including Lyon Phelps, Richard Eberhart, and Richard Wilbur), Gorey was a founding member of the Poets' Theater, an ill-attended but nevertheless influential forerunner of the New York Artists' Theater. It opened in 1951 (a year after Gorey's graduation); one of its first productions was *Try, Try*, a play by O'Hara. The sets were by Gorey; the stars were Ashbery and Lang.

Gorey's prodigal consumption of culture had already begun. While Harvard was teaching the staid classics, Gorey and his companions were exploring French Surrealism, Japanese Kabuki and Noh, Hollywood "guilty pleasures," and, above all, the perfumed, semi-satirical fictions of English novelists like Ronald Firbank, Evelyn Waugh, Ivy Compton-Burnett, C. Day-Lewis, and Henry Green.[6] "They were a counter-culture, an early and élitist form of it," says the writer Brad Gooch, author of the biography of Frank O'Hara, *City Poet*. "Before he met Gorey, O'Hara was a pretty earnest kid, but Gorey had this nonsensical style that came from his Anglophilia, from the English books that he read. So that kind of *Brideshead Revisited* sensibility was what Gorey conveyed to O'Hara. They were inventing this alternative culture, and you always had to choose something that wasn't accepted by the mainstream. Gorey was a big Ivy Compton-Burnett fan, whereas O'Hara was more inclined to C. Day-Lewis. And O'Hara liked Rimbaud, and Bunny Lang preferred Auden. So there were these little tiny distinctions that meant everything. And this attitude has stuck with all of them."

You can see it still in Gorey's work. The solemn and isolated Victorian households in which terrible deeds unfold seem to bear the stamp of Ivy Compton-Burnett (who wrote about little else); the wry, yet convoluted Briticisms remind one of Firbank's sublime nonsense; the peculiar austerity of some of Gorey's drawings, in which he sacrifices his insistent wood grains and wallpapers to floods of white space, owes a lot to the Japanese art and literature he loves. There is also a marked strain of French Surrealism in his work. Edmund Wilson detected it in 1959, in a *New Yorker* piece, which was the first important critical notice Gorey received.[7] Wilson was referring to Gorey's fourth album, *The Object-Lesson*, a series of dream-like non-sequiturs:

> On the shore a bat, or possibly an umbrella,
> disengaged itself from the shrubbery,
> causing those nearby to recollect the miseries of childhood.
> It now became apparent (despite the lack of library paste)
> that something had happened to the vicar;
> guns began to go off in the distance.

Lines like those are reminiscent of such avant-garde techniques as the "cut up," whereby William Burroughs and Brion Gysin[8] created bizarre nonsense sentences by scissoring newspaper strips and rearranging them randomly. The Surrealists had done something similar with their *cadavre-exquis* experiments, in which someone would write a phrase on a sheet of paper, fold it over to hide part of it, and pass it on to the next person, who would in turn concoct the next piece of the phrase, and so forth. (They made visual *cadavres*, too.) Clifford Ross has pointed out the *cadavre-exquis* quality of some of Gorey's work, but Gorey is tied more closely to meaning than his predecessors were. He finds a meeting ground between the Surrealists and the Japanese, who allow silence to create meaning by letting the reader fill in what's left out. Gorey's books demand participation.

"I'm beginning to feel that if you create something, you're killing a lot of other things," Gorey says. "And the way I write, since I do leave out most of the connections, and very little is pinned down, I feel that I'm doing a minimum of damage to other possibilities that might arise in a reader's mind. The authors I dislike the most or find unreadable are the ones who are forcing a personality on me that I don't really care very much for in the first place. And they also tend to be the writers who are completely exhaustive about whatever it is they're writing about until you're just left feeling 'O.K., you've nailed me to the chair, that's it, there's nothing left to think about, nothing left to question.' I think of my least favorite writers in the world—Thomas Mann is high on the list. I dutifully read *The Magic Mountain* and felt as if I had t.b. for a year afterward. But my least favorite author in all the world— how *could* I have forgotten? Henry James. I hate Henry James more than tongue can tell. I have read everything he wrote, sometimes more than once. I think he's the worst writer in the English language. Those endless sentences. I always pick up Henry James and I think, *Oooh!* This is *won*derful! And then I will hear a little sound. And it's the plug being pulled. And the whole thing is going down the drain like the bathwater."

Gorey retains most of the tastes he exhibited at Harvard, though his range and knowledge—especially of movies and ballet—expanded when he moved to New York in 1953. Through a Radcliffe friend, Barbara Zimmerman, he met the editor and publisher Jason Epstein, her future husband; Epstein was launching a new division of Doubleday called Anchor Books, publishing out-of-print classics in a format that would come to be known as the trade paperback. Gorey wound up drawing most of the jackets. "They were beautiful, ravishing," recalls Barbara Epstein, now the co-editor of *The New York Review of Books*. "He worked very slowly, with a tremendous perfectionism, and he would never let a drawing out of his hands if it was less than perfect." Seven years later, Gorey joined Jason Epstein in starting the Looking Glass Library, an Anchor-style division of Random House that published classics of children's literature in hard cover. After Looking Glass dissolved, Gorey spent an unhappy year at Bobbs-Merrill, and by the time he lost that job, amid some internecine turmoil, in 1963, he was ready to give up the workaday world for good. "I had so much free-lance work—book covers, and so forth and so on—that I didn't really have time to look for another job," he says. Besides, he wanted to devote more time to his own books.

By now, he has published some eighty of them, and he has notebooks full of stories and poems that he hasn't got around to illustrating yet. He still takes on illustration jobs, and he has also begun to stage small theatrical productions of his own on Cape Cod, adapting them himself from his published and unpublished work, and directing his own gaggle of amateur actors in them. On the whole, despite his solitude, he seems quite content, just as he always has. Which makes the darkness and terror in his work all the more puzzling.

I decide to ask him about it once more, and this time, in his meandering way, he gives me something like an answer. "You know, Jane

Austen, at the end of *Mansfield Park*, said that famous thing: 'Let other pens dwell on guilt and misery. I quit such odious subjects as soon as I can.' Well, if you really analyze that, it doesn't mean that she has not been writing about guilt and misery. She's written about it only to the extent that it's absolutely necessary to get it across. And as soon as she's got it across she's just not going to wallow in it. I mean, my favorite genre is the sinister-slash-cozy. I think there should be a little bit of uneasiness in everything, because I do think we're all really in a sense living on the edge. So much of life is inexplicable. Inexplicable things happen to me, things that are so inexplicable that I'm not even sure that something happened. And you suddenly think, 'Well, if that could happen, anything could happen.' One moment, something is there, and then, the next, it is not there. One minute, both of my feet are perfectly all right, and then, a minute later, somebody has dropped a fifty-pound weight on one of them, and now suddenly I've got an injured foot and I have to go do something about this injured-foot thing. The things that happen to you are usually the things that you haven't thought of or that come absolutely out of nowhere. And all you can do is cope with them when they turn up."

This last may be the principle on which he has based his life as well as his art. The world is uncertain, beyond control; it leaks and lurches, and only a panoply of compulsions and stylizations can begin to combat the disorder. When I ask him about the obsessive cross-hatching in his work, he replies. "It's partly insecurity. I mean, where do you leave off? Where do you allow the white space to intervene?" Gorey has invented a life for himself in which it almost never does.

But that life seems to have fed him. "Oh dear," he says. "There are so many things we're brought up to believe that it takes you an awfully long time to realize that they aren't you." Suddenly, his voice goes bossy and falsetto, as though he were imitating some all-purpose Midwestern schoolmarm. "Why don't you travel? Why don't you get a master's degree in . . . something? Why don't you try doing this, that, or the other? Well, you're probably not doing it because it's not right. Why worry about it? God knows, there's enough to worry about without worrying about worrying about things."

He toys with the cat's tail. "You know, Ted Shawn, the choreographer—he used to say, 'When in doubt, twirl.' Oh I do think that's such a great line."

# Edward Gorey

Simon Henwood,
*Purr*, Spring 1995

When I look at the books and the stories, they have this feeling that they are like silent movies.

Some of them have been consciously inspired by silent films. I think basically I kind of think in a silent-film way. I think, looking back, I was seeing an awful lot of silent films and everything when I was starting out publicly, as it were. I think I tended to look at lots of film stills and so I think that I began to draw people that way, and pick up costumes and backgrounds, and basically I think the greatest influence on my work is the French film director Louis Feuillade.[1]

I mean I haven't seen that much of Feuillade but *The Fantômas* and *The Vampires*, *Tih-Minh*, and probably the greatest movie ever made,

which I've only seen once. It's called *Barrabas*, and I think it was more or less his last silent crime serial (about 1918 or '19). I always remember it as the greatest movie I ever saw.

**Your characters seem to be more like catalysts for cautionary tales. The players seem like strangers and almost passing acquaintances, and it seems you avoid invading the living human spirit in favor of using people rather like props, almost like dolls.**

Well, I hadn't thought of it that way. I tend to think of it in terms of plot is everything, even in the things of mine that don't have a plot. I mean, like limericks and things, and very short verses, to me they're all a plot even if it's hardly present at all. But to me, I suppose if you're doing anything that short, and relying, or hanging everything on the plot, then there isn't much room for character development or whatever.

For my work, I'm not terribly interested in things that I am interested in personally, like the Victorian novel or things that I can't use in my work very much. Somebody was asking me why I never did landscape; actually I'm really quite obsessed with landscape, but I really wouldn't know how to deal with it in my work, so I don't. Or very seldom.

**It seems a very interesting mix: you obviously have an interest in Victorian literature, but also the Japanese Noh-theater and the whole idea of things being left out. So, on one hand, there's an immense amount of detail, but on the other, some of the most fundamental points of the plot are left open.**

Well, that's probably because I didn't know how to cope. I mean, I would love to be able to write a big Victorian novel, though I think the big pseudo-Victorian novels that get written now are not the same thing.

The trouble is, I can get interested in just about anything, which really amounts to being interested in nothing! I mean, I have very eclectic tastes and whatnot, and people tend to say "Oh my God, you've read everything, because we never mention anything that you don't know something about." Probably. I know very little about it, but I've read something about it.

I have periods—about a year ago I got interested in Jung, and I've been working my way through the books of Jung, all sorts of books that are based on Jung, and people who are influenced by him and whatnot. Then lately, I've gotten back onto things like Eliade,[2] the "comparative religion" guy, and I've read a lot of him at one point or another some time ago, and now I'm working my way through all the Eliade books I haven't read. I think I'm about to have a spasm on Greek mythology because I'm reading the latest chic book on the subject, *The Marriage of Cadmos and Harmony* by some Italian author whose name I can't remember.[3] Anyway, it's a complete redoing of Greek mythology in very bizarre terming, with very bizarre modern terms, and coming across things I've never heard of before, like at one point Orestes was so upset by the Furies pursuing him, and at that time they were all black, that he bit off one of the fingers of his left hand, at which point the Furies all turned white! I've never heard this before! But the book is filled with dippy little anecdotes like that. I keep thinking, how can I use that?

And since I've been living up here especially, at some point or other I succumbed to television, so there I am, parked in front of the television more often than not, making stuffed animals or reading or drawing, or writing, but since I don't go to New York any more I buy endless things from catalogues, and the number of art books I have is getting higher and higher and higher, and I've never gotten rid of all my LPs, and then I got into cassettes, and now I'm on CDs and I get practically every catalogue issued. CDs are particularly entertaining because you keep coming across all these composers that no one's ever heard of! Half the things in the catalogue seem to be "And this is the first recording of so-and-so!"

**One unique thing about your drawings and your stories is the way you convey a sense of melancholy. And that the stories convey a feeling of shock and often of menace, but are never threatening.**

For some reason, I do like making people feel faintly uneasy about the whole thing. I suppose because I think life is more than faintly unsettling. I tend to have more of a reputation for the macabre, that I think is more than justified. . . .

**But you wouldn't call it horror, would you?**

No, the things that really horrify me I really wouldn't put into it. The closest thing that really horrified me, and really affected me, was *The Loathsome Couple,* which was based on the Moors murderers. I read Pamela Hansford-Johnson's[4] book on it; I'd followed it in the papers. And that I found truly horrifying.

I mean, there are some Victorian cases that are truly horrifying too, but there was a different way of writing about things in those days. I've got a vast library of famous murder cases and whatnot, and I'm working on a puppet play about Lizzie Borden at the moment. I've done my share of reading about all that. But most of the True Crime now that gets printed, especially in paperback, is a lot more lurid. Ghastly sets of people. It really does not have the something or other that it had before, in the Victorian cases, or even in the Twenties.

**I had picked out *The Loathsome Couple* as one that had a gruesome subject, but even so, you don't feel shocked. It's almost like taking mild amusement, an uneasy pleasure in it.**

It's funny, because now when I read it I find it kind of amusing, in a rather odd way, needless to remark. But I've always thought one of my best inventions was that ghastly meal they had that consisted of artificial grape soda and a couple of other awful things. I thought up the worst things I could possibly think of, and I showed it to my editor at the time, and he didn't think it was very funny, and I thought, "Oh really, dear, I don't think it's very funny either; what made you think that I thought it was funny?"

And there was the counter-culture paper down in SoHo for a while *The SoHo Weekly News.* I'd done one book for them and they were badgering me for another one, and I thought, "Oh, knock it off. I'm going to do this, just to be snobby!" Actually, I think they're some of the

At times they said they had done it all, but other times they denied everything.

best drawings I've ever done. From an aesthetic point of view, it's quite brilliant! It appeared serially over thirty weeks, I think it was, and my editor, Peter Weed, said, "Can we have it as a book after it's been serialized?" And I said, "Well, Peter, I don't think you want it!" And he said, "Oh, of course we want it!" and oh well, O.K. It was the one book that we did get a little reaction from; I remember how one bookstore—it was either the University of New Hampshire or the University of Vermont, sent back the copies they'd ordered with a very revealing letter saying "We think this book is absolutely revolting. Everyone in the store has read it and we refuse to carry it!"

What really baffled me, and I'm still baffled by it, is that when *Gorey Stories* was [produced] a few years later, [*The Loathsome Couple*] was the second act. I thought, "They're out of their tiny minds. What made them think you could put this on the stage?" Maybe it was just me, except it was the funniest part of the show. Do not ask me how this was done, because the two people that did *The Loathsome Couple* were absolutely brilliant, just really transcended doing it. But they did it absolutely seriously. I mean, it was horrifying, but I guess it was so over the top that all you could do was just kinda roll on the floor.

I've sometimes toyed with the idea of staging it myself, and I don't quite know how, although I would like to tour with it some time, just to see what would happen.

**One of the other themes I've noticed running through the books is a fascination with things that are lost, not so much mislaid, but really lost forever.**

You've really studied this all much more than I have!

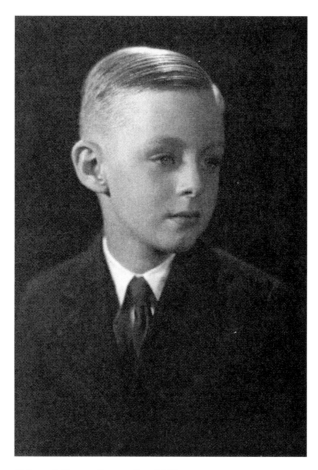

Edward Gorey, September, 1932

**I was wondering, as a child were you always missing, or were you a bit previous?**

When I look back on my childhood I have an extraordinarily warped view of it, when I really stop to think of it. I like to think of myself as, "Oh here was this sensitive child, an only child, who was not misunderstood or anything, but I mean somehow I didn't." And when I look back and think, "Well, then, why I was always out with a bunch of other children? And why were we always doing this and that?" And so on. And this somehow doesn't fit my image!

We moved around a lot when I was a child; I never quite understood that. I mean, at one point I skipped two grades at Grammar School, but I went to five different Grammar Schools, so I was always changing schools, it seemed to me, when I was at Grammar School, which I didn't like.

I hated moving, and we were always doing it. Sometimes we just moved a block away into another apartment; it was all very weird. But then I look back and try to figure out what my family was like and I'm completely blank on the subject. I mean, I could never write an autobiography because I wouldn't have the slightest idea of what to say about anything.

Occasionally, like when I roomed with Frank O'Hara at Harvard for a few years, and when that big biography of Frank[5] was being written up, the author used to call me and ask me this and that, and sometimes I could remember and sometimes I couldn't.

Whenever someone asks me about the people I've known, I don't want to talk about it. The more I think about it, I think that if I tried to put it into words it would become so completely distorted that it might as well not exist at all. So I refuse to try and talk about it. Basically, I distrust language.

**Do you think your work is humor laced with tragedy, or tragedy laced with humor?**

Oh, I would prefer not to think of it as either one. I would prefer to think of it as all seamless. In a way, I think style is everything. And I'm always vaguely irritated by, say, Shakespeare going from tragedy to comic relief. I'd much rather have the whole thing there at once.

Actually, one of the things I most admire is this Japanese movie director called Naruse,[6] who I think of along with Feuillade (not that he's a really great influence on me). He died back in the Sixties, I guess. He started out directing silent movies, and from what little I've read about him, he was one of those directors who never told anyone anything. He would just say, "Get up here in front of the camera," and his movies are very low key. Do you know Ozu's[7] stuff? Well, they're not quite as low key; whenever I see an Ozu movie I think, "Oh God, somebody has nailed my knees to the floor." The way it's "here's the establishing shot outdoors," "here's the establishing shot indoors," and from then on you're just kneeling in front of the whole thing and the camera never moves, never does anything.

Well, Naruse's movies are a bit like that. There's usually an establishing shot outdoors and one indoors, and the camera very seldom moves, and there are no pyrotechnics; the photography is nice but it doesn't call attention to itself or anything. And most of his movies are all about domestic situations; usually women tend to be the protagonists.

The first movie of his I ever saw—there was a period in New York, there was a Buddhist temple that was on 94th or 95th Street on the West Side, which was in an old brownstone. And they showed Japanese movies on the weekend: they'd have Friday night, Saturday night, and Sunday matinée shows. And somehow a friend of mine discovered they were doing this and we went up and at that period, I think most of the movies were imported from the West Coast. But a lot of them had no subtitles, which made it quite fascinating sometimes. Actually the Japanese used to complain about this, because a lot of them didn't speak Japanese well enough.

But they used to show a Samurai movie, usually, then a domestic, contemporary one, or a period one. And I remember there was one glorious three-hour domestic movie—we used to be there for four or five hours, sometimes longer—one night that had a father and a mother and they had about ten children and everybody, I mean everybody, including a couple of servants, was involved in triangles. So there were about thirty or forty characters and none of us had the faintest idea what was going on. We were like "Do you think he's sleeping with her?" Of course, with that many Japanese people, it's not terribly easy to keep track of them all.

But anyway, the first Naruse movie I ever saw was about three aging geisha who were retired, and they used to see each other all the time and they had children and they had boyfriends and ex-husbands. And it was maybe about a two-hour movie, and it was kind of fascinating. It didn't bother you that you didn't really know where this was going, it was just interesting moment to moment. All the acting was absolutely wonderful and it was interesting from a sociological point of view. It was kind of like *The Golden Girls* or something; they would dither around with each other and help each other out and things.

And in the very last scene, one of their children was going off on a train, so all three ladies get dressed up and go see off whoever it was, and as they're walking back home, they're going across a bridge and they suddenly just break loose and start dancing and laughing and singing, and that was the end. It was called *Late Blooming Chrysanthemums* or something very metaphorical.

Suddenly the whole movie came together and you realized that you had seen this wonderful slice of life, that everything connected with everything else, and it was really heart-rending. Some of his movies are more blatantly heart-rending, because he makes terrible things happen to people. But you really had a sense of life as it is lived.

**If there was a period or a culture that you would most identify with, or embrace, would it be the Japanese?**

Oh probably, because, apart from Jane Austen, who is my favorite author in a way, I'm also absolutely ga-ga over *The Tale of Genji*, which I've read six or seven times in the Arthur Waley translation; I've read the Seidensticker translation once, twice I guess, to try to compare them.[8]

**What is it about it that you love so much?**

I don't know. I mean, it took me years to get through *The Tale of Genji*. I think I first started it when I went to work at Doubleday in 1953. For one thing, the format of the Waley translation is very bad, because the lines are too close together and too long to read comfortably, so that you have to keep doing this with your finger or you keep losing your place. So it took a long time to get into, there are endless numbers of characters, and a lot of it is quite inexplicable. I mean, I find it very difficult to remember what everybody was doing, but I finally got through it back in the early Fifties and I re-read it every couple of years.

I think it's really the greatest novel ever written. I have this theory that the best things are always right at the beginning, 'cause it's practically the first novel ever written. And it's peculiar, because who knows what the book is really like? Only the Japanese.

I mean there's some famous contemporary writer who has translated *The Tale of Genji* three times into modern Japanese, because the Japanese themselves can't read it, and everybody says that the most extreme criticism of the Waley translation is that Waley read *The Tale of Genji* and then wrote another book himself! Actually, it's very strange because he left out bits of it here and there; in fact, he leaves out one chapter for reasons he never explained to anyone. But the Seidensticker translation, which is supposedly much more authentic, is actually much shorter than the Waley translation. The Waley translation is, I think, one of the greatest pieces of English prose ever perpetrated. I can read it over and over because I think one tends to distort really good stuff in one's mind, or it's got so much in it that one time you will latch on to some aspect of it or other and it will seem more meaningful.

**Often, some of your pictures don't even relate, or appear to relate at all to the sentences.**

Actually, one of my projects, which I've never quite gotten around to doing, is two books in which the pictures for one were printed with the text for the other and vice versa. And I should probably do it a couple of years apart, so that somebody would really have to make an effort. And then, if you did put them together, there wouldn't be that much basically. I don't think I ever got around to writing the text for these. The older I've gotten, the more I've tended to like things you can fiddle around with. I don't know whether you've seen that little pack of cards that I created. . . .

**Yes, you mean the pack where each card has an image and a sentence in which you can make a cohesive story no matter what combination you lay them out in. There must be billions. . . .**

Oh it's incredible, and I've got another I'm writing, although I know what the drawings are going to look like; instead of the cards all having the same back there will be alternative versions of the things on the back of the cards, so that then you'll have an even more incredible number. That one with the cards, I tend to use them on the stage; I shuffle them at random, write them out, and then we do them all. Somewhere I've got a list of ways they are connected, and some of them are completely unconnected, and so forth and so on.

**I love *The Dancing Rock*.**

Yeah, well I was in my minimalist period with *The Dancing Rock* and *The Floating Elephant*, and then *Nature and Art,* which I think is my ultimate philosophical statement. Everybody sort of looks at it and says, "What? The pointless book." To me it says everything about the relation in literature between nature and art.

# Edward Gorey: Portrait of the Artist in Chilling Color

Scott Baldauf,

*The Christian Science Monitor*, 31 October 1996

Yarmouth Port, Mass.
    Edward Gorey sits on the steps of his sunny porch, doodling in a notebook. He's a tall bald man with a neatly trimmed white beard. He is dressed casually in jeans and a sweatshirt, and wears an ornate Ethiopian crucifix around his neck. We shake hands, and I marvel that such a large hand, as thick as a bricklayer's, covered with heavy brass rings, is capable of such delicate, subtle art.

    "My first drawings came at the age of one and a half," he says as we drive to his favorite lunch spot, Jack's Out Back, "and I hasten to add

**Edward Gorey and friend at Yarmouth Port, Massachusetts**

that they showed no talent whatever. Looking back, it's all a mystery . . . I just drifted into this."

Like the famed film director Alfred Hitchcock, Gorey creates tension by suggesting violence, rather than showing it. Inanimate legs jut out from underneath shrubs or out of doorways, and the only hint that something awful has happened comes in a wry footnote. Gorey knows when to leave things unsaid. He wishes modern film directors had the same subtle touch.

"I can sit through an endless amount of violence, but I think [today's movies] have gone too far," he says. "But then, I'm the sort of person who thinks that movies went downhill after World War I. Basically, when sound came in." His favorite movie is the silent picture *Vampyr*, by the late Danish director Carl Dreyer.[1] "You don't see a thing and yet it's the most chilling movie I have ever seen," he says. "I think your own imagination does a better job."

In his private life, Gorey is a complex jumble of contradictions. He reads murder mysteries and watches action pictures, but avoids movies where animals come to harm. He delivers punch lines and sardonic commentary with ease, but rarely laughs. "I don't set out to be funny," he says. "Obviously, if I find myself giggling about something, I'll keep it in." Referring to *The Gashlycrumb Tinies*, he quips, "I must say I did think at the time that 'N is for Neville who died of ennui' was rather fetching."

New ideas come all the time from friends, novels, and even television. One current project in Gorey's notebook is a puppet show that turns Puccini's opera *Madame Butterfly* on its head. In Gorey's version, [Butterfly] is an American girl from the Midwest who falls in love with a traveling Japanese businessman.

"You'd think I just moved here, but I've been here ten years," Gorey says as he guides us through the gantlet of boxes and objets d'art. Gorey has what he calls a "yard-sale mentality," and the books that don't fit into the shelves of his living room remain stacked in boxes on his couch, his desk, and on any other available surface. It is here that his six cats—Charles, George, Weedums, Alice, Thomas, and Jane—are on perpetual prowl.

A calico jumps into my lap ("Hello, Jane") and a ginger cat jumps into his ("Hello, Charles") and I ask the life-long bachelor whom he is closest to. "My cats," he says, hugging Charles. "There are a few people I see all the time. But when I'm really working I'd rather not see people that much, and when I'm not working, I'd like to have that time to myself. I have to make an effort to be social."

To be sure, Yarmouth Port makes a perfect town for a recluse, but Gorey seems determined to bring a bit of Gotham to the Cape. Working with a half-dozen local amateurs, he writes puppet shows and musical reviews with titles like *Crazed Teacups* or *Blithering Christmas*[2] and shows them in various seaside communities. This may seem like charity work for someone of Gorey's stature, but he reminds me that his adaptation of *Dracula* also got its start as community theater.

As Gorey and I speak, Jane gets up and trades places with Charles, who sneezes onto my notebook. Charles stretches out, and seems to imply that my note taking is far less important than giving him a vigorous scratch behind the ears. It occurs to me that the cats are much like Gorey, who calls himself "easily distracted."

By now my questions have dwindled and Gorey leads me to the door. I ask him if he misses New York and he answers with a story. "I remember sitting in one of those Greek diners," he says. "I thought, 'There are more people passing this window than Jane Austen saw in her entire life. What good is this doing me?'"

# The Gorey Details

David Streitfeld,

*The Washington Post Book World*, 14 September 1997

V ery early one summer morning, Edward Gorey awoke to a crash-
ing noise in the next room. He yelled at the cats to knock it off.
Presently, there was another crash. The cats never listen. Gorey went
back to sleep. When he finally got up and looked, it turned out part of
the ceiling had fallen in.

That gives a slightly exaggerated idea of what the artist's Cape Cod
house is like. It's not all decaying, just cluttered. Boxes are piled up, as if
he had just moved in. (He's lived here for more than a decade.) The
cats—five at the moment—have the run of the place. There are books
everywhere, long runs of all sorts of authors. Gorey says he is cleaning
up, moving the books out to the barn, having some repairs done to that

antiquated roof, but there is a sense that it's all a losing battle. As every book lover knows, volumes expand to fill all the available space, then they hide.

Recently, for instance, Gorey ordered from New York a copy of V. S. Pritchett's book on Turgenev *The Gentle Barbarian: The Life and Work of Turgenev,* "About three weeks ago I looked down on the floor and there was another copy of it, and then a week ago I looked somewhere else and there was another copy, and I thought 'Do I really need three?'"

But like all true book fanatics, Gorey is reluctant to let anything go. As soon as he tries, he thinks: I might want to read this sometime. It happens, too. After a staged reading of *The Seagull*, he thought it was time to go back to Chekhov.

"I discovered I had the collected short stories that were reissued a while ago, and a dozen other volumes by him. So now I'm working my way through. And as someone put it, when you're reading Chekhov, you wonder why you ever read anyone else. It's uncanny, simply because you can't quite figure out how he manages to do it. I'm a great one for marking passages discreetly, with a little dot, but with Chekhov I finish and I find I didn't mark anything. In a sense, it's written mostly in clichés. There's no endless search for the right word, which I find so fatiguing in Mr. Flaubert, but you come to the end of a Chekhov story and find it's almost unbearably moving."

Some of this commentary resembles what people have been saying about Gorey almost since his first book, *The Unstrung Harp*, appeared in 1953. His style is inimitable and immediately recognizable, but the effect is famously hard to describe. Macabre yet delicate; grim but amusing; ghoulish without a drop of blood. Next month, Harcourt Brace is reissuing *The Curious Sofa* and *The Gashlycrumb Tinies*; the first, in particular, is a classic, a send-up of '20s pornography that never uses a naughty word. (Sample line: "Alice, quite exhausted, was helped to bed by Lady Celia's French maid, Lise, whom she found delightfully sympathetic.")

These works were done thirty-six and thirty-four years ago, respectively, but there is neither early nor late Gorey. "I was probably fully formed by the time I was twenty-one or twenty-two," he says. Just don't ask him how he came to be this way. He was an only child, born in 1925, but says there was nothing aberrant about his upbringing; it's worth mentioning, however, that *Goreography*, a useful bibliography/price guide issued last year, says the artist "tested poison gas" while in the Army during World War II.

**Edward Gorey at Gotham Book Mart, New York**

*Photographer: Bill Yoscary*

Gorey was pervasive almost from the beginning. The only real job he held for any length was working for Anchor Books from 1953 until 1960; he designed the covers for many paperback classics, some of which remained widely available until 1970 or so, and can be found in secondhand bookstores—although not after I've been there.

As Gorey examined some of the Anchors, he said he had forgotten his own artwork. He's done so much that this is probably inevitable. He gazed at a copy of *What Maisie Knew*. "My Henry Jameses were thought to be terribly good, probably because hate is as powerful as love, and I hate Henry James more than anybody. I hear they just made a movie out of *The Wings of the Dove* with my least favorite actress of all time, Helena Bonham Carter. I find her lack of a neck very off-putting and especially her acting."

Gorey would much rather talk about actors, books, or writers than art. "I've always liked detective stories. They're interesting the way true crime is interesting: you find out how people live. But all the detective writers I used to read are dead, or else have gotten so arty I can't bear them any more, like P. D. James." He thinks Agatha Christie is due considerable respect. "She didn't overwrite, she didn't underwrite, she moved right along, she's endlessly entertaining, she's ingenious— occasionally a little too ingenious, but what the hell. Sometimes I remember them halfway through. Sometimes I get to the last chapter and wonder, 'Is this how it came out last time?'"

After talking to Gorey for a while, you begin to feel he has read everything, even people long since forgotten. *Especially* people long since forgotten. "Have you reached the age where books disappear all of a sudden? In secondhand bookstores I used to think, 'Do I want to read the entire works of Gilbert Canaan?[1] Because here they are.' So I would open one, read a couple of sentences and think, 'No.' And then I suddenly come across a reference and think, 'Oh, I'll go get some Gilbert

Canaan,' and there's zip. Does anyone know who Charles Morgan[2] was anymore?"

Not me.

"An English middlebrow novelist who wrote some Book-of-the-Month-Club-type bestsellers in the '30s," the artist kindly explains. "Charles Morgan was for people who couldn't quite get through Virginia Woolf. But now I think he's gone."

Gorey has all this time to read because he lives alone with the cats. The longtime New Yorker has turned his back on the city. "The last few times I was down there, I even rattled around in my own apartment. There wasn't much I wanted to do. But it's probably getting to me that there's nobody to talk to up here."

He thinks for a bit. "Although I'm not a great one for expecting people to talk about anything I'm interested in." Which is odd, because he's interested in everything from schlock horror movies such as *Spawn* ("Why was I stupid enough to see it? It was all in the trailer.") to the local news. His one semblance of social life comes from a visit to the local cafe for breakfast. On his return, he gets down to work on one of his many projects. Theoretically. In reality, he confesses, "I have a little nap, usually, then see what's on CNN."

No wonder Gorey, while famously productive, is famously behind. "I haven't done a major book"—and he stops to mock himself, repeating "a major book?" and giving one of his big falsetto laughs—"since *The Raging Tide* in 1987, I guess. But I've whipped up a lot of little stuff the past couple of years. I used to worry I'd never have any more ideas and I'd dry up, and now I think, 'Oh God, if only I would.' "

# Edward Gorey:
# Proust Questionnaire

Anonymous,

*Vanity Fair*, October 1997

**W**hat is your idea of perfect happiness?
Sky, water, light.

**What is your current state of mind?**
Changeable.

**What or who is the greatest love of your life?**
Cats.

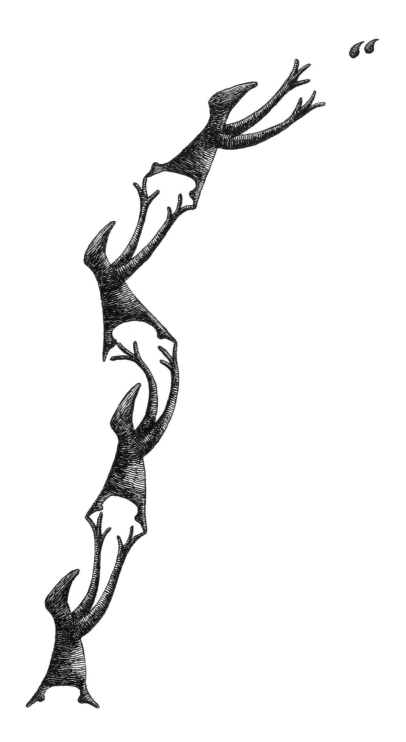

**What are your favorite names?**

Filboid Studge, Fantômas, Astérix.

**Which living person do you most admire?**

Balthus.

One piddling question remains.

**Which living person do you most despise?**

Where to begin . . .

**Who are your heroes in real life?**

George Balanchine, Lincoln Kirstein, Frances Steloff.

**What is the trait you most deplore in yourself?**

Stupidity.

**What is the trait you most deplore in others?**

Cruelty.

**What is your greatest extravagance?**

Buying things at yard sales.

**What is your most treasured possession?**

The one most recently acquired.

**What is it that you most dislike?**

The results of fear and greed.

**What do you consider your greatest achievement?**

I hope that it is still to come.

**What is your favorite journey?**

Looking out the window.

**What is your favorite occupation?**

Drifting.

**What is your most marked characteristic?**

Dither.

**What do you regard as the lowest depth of misery?**

I think I still have to find out what it is.

**What is your greatest regret?**

That I don't have one.

**When and where were you happiest?**

Whatever I said would not be true.

**On what occasion do you lie?**

Almost any.

**Which talent would you most like to have?**

Any to do with music or dance.

**What do you dislike most about your appearance?**

Everything but my toes.

**If you could change one thing about yourself, what would it be?**

To be able to say no.

**If you could change one thing about your family, what would it be?**

To live with cats who are a tad less loopy.

**How would you like to die?**

Unexpectedly in my sleep.

**If you were to die and come back as a person or thing, what do you think it would be?**

A stone.

**If you could choose what to come back as, what would it be?**

A neutrino.

**What is your motto?**

O the of it all.

# A Gorey Encounter

Ed Pinsent,

*Speak*, Fall 1997

I know your stories from the anthology volumes *Amphigorey*, *Amphigorey Too*, and *Amphigorey Also*. But they existed as small run books before this. Are books like art objects to you?

I've done a lot of these little books that I've published myself. It's nice to have [the anthologies] but I'd prefer that everybody could see the original books. I'm not a great one for art books that cost several hundred dollars, printed on gorgeous paper. I don't think my work lends itself to that very well.

*TUH* is over, so to speak, but far from done with. The galleys have arrived, and Mr Earbrass goes over them with mingled excitement and disgust. It all looks so different set up in type that at first he thought they had sent him the wrong ones by mistake. He is quite giddy from trying to physically control the sheets and at the same time keep the amount of absolutely necessary changes within the allowed pecuniary limits.

**Do you consider yourself a writer more than an artist?**

If push comes to shove I consider myself more of a writer. For the last ten years I've mainly done theater, so now there are three of me—the writer, the artist, and the theater person. Somebody put together some of my old pieces and did a theater piece that wasn't exactly a raging success, but it was interesting and I got the bug myself, kind of. When I started writing years ago, the first things I wrote were plays. I hope the world will never see them. Apparently I must have had a leaning toward theater at the very beginning and I didn't follow it up. I started out putting together things of my own that I'd already written, then using material that was otherwise unpublished, and for the last couple years I've been writing directly for the theater.

**The way you arrange information within a drawing strikes me as theatrical.**

Probably even more like movies, because I've been going to see movies ever since I could walk, practically. I don't go nearly as much anymore since it's all gone down the tubes.

**What was the last play you staged?**

At the moment I am doing something called *Epistolary Play,* which is two people reading letters. I thought there was a faint possibility someone may want to do it sometime. All it takes is two chairs and two people. Every time I see another production of *Love Letters* . . . Is it as popular in England as it is in America?

**I don't know *Love Letters*, sorry.**

Oh, I'm so glad to hear that. To be perfectly frank, it's like a disease. It's a play for two characters by A. R. Gurney. He writes sort of middle-brow, genteel, half-comedy, half-tragedy things, which are very popular here because they exactly mirror how the theater-going audience fancies itself. He did *Love Letters,* which only takes a man and a woman [to perform]. It's the history of their lives in letters. Any two people, one man and one woman, can do it at the drop of a hat, and here on Cape Cod, whose population is well under 200,000, it gets done about five times a year. It's a perfectly appalling piece of gibberish. Anyway, one day I thought, "Oh the hell with all this. I'm going to write a two-character play that people can read sitting in chairs." Needless to remark, it turned out to be something quite difficult, and almost impossible to follow. I opened it last week. I have a group [of actors] that I've been working with for ten years now.

**So you oversee the productions as well?**

Oh, I do that. I do everything. I'd hum along if I could carry a tune. When I'm illustrating somebody's work nobody dares come near me, because I say, "I'm going to do it this way." It's perfectly clear that I do not relish suggestions as to what to draw, or anything else! I discovered working in the theater that I'm completely the opposite of what everybody would think of me as being—telling everybody exactly what to do and how to do it. I hardly direct at all. I just let everybody carry on and hope that osmosis will get what I have in mind. And it really doesn't matter if they do; in fact, that's why I rather like working in the theater —because you never know what's going to happen.

**Are you satisfied with the results?**

Yes, I'm always absolutely enthralled by it. But it's a very odd situation—all the people that I've been working with have daytime jobs. They don't get paid [for acting]. All of them are exceptionally talented but I don't think they're psychologically capable of working in a real commercial-type theater. We've never done more than twelve performances. By the time the twelfth performance is over, it's changed beyond all recognition and gone in different directions.

**So it changes organically as it goes along?**

Oh yes, that's the thing. If you're doing commercial theater you have to reproduce something more or less the same, night after night. Yes, we're organic, like some strange amoeba pushing about under the microscope. It's always fascinating. This play I just wrote, I still don't have the faintest idea what it's about. After two performances some of it is beginning to make a bit of sense to me.

**Is there an element of catharsis, of strong emotion in this work?**

Oh no. If you have to use one word, they're probably Dada more than anything else.

**Are you interested in Dada?**

Yes. I regret that I wasn't around when it was [happening]. I'm also very interested in Surrealism. I think most of the stuff that was produced was not terribly interesting. All you have to do is hand me a book of Surrealist short stories and I go to sleep instantly. The art is marginally more interesting. The whole theory of Surrealism I'm all for. And even more so Dada. By the time you get to the Surrealists, they're getting more philosophical.

**In your stories, I've always sensed an element of extreme cruelty bubbling up, yet a refusal to show violence directly.**

I guess. I don't know. I've discovered with these plays—the characterization is minimal, the plot is really odd. We've been using puppets which I design and make, so the whole thing is kind of superficial and giddy. But occasionally things come out I wouldn't have thought were in there, but apparently they are, because that's what happens.

**Do you ever think about the effect your work has on readers?**

Oh, well, in a way I hope it's mildly unsettling. The whole question with audiences, and especially with theater, is one I find very strange. I had to do some acting in a show when somebody came down with spinal meningitis. I was the only person who knew the part, of course, because I had written the damn thing. I acted for about a week and was totally at sea. It was a very mysterious experience. I'd become absolutely bodiless or something. I have no conception of what I'm doing out there, though I realized that my acting was getting better.

For years I attended the New York City Ballet, and I've always said it all depends what night the performance was. It never had anything to do with the performance, what the audience response was. As far as I'm concerned, the audience should be completely ignored, but the actors like to hear people giggling and carrying on out there. I tell them, "You're going to get huge applause at the end," and I'm always right, but they still can't help wishing for the immediate response. I suppose that's why they're actors.

**Is there any kind of personal dimension to your stories?**

There are probably lots of them, but I've never found my own reactions particularly interesting, [not] even to myself, I must say. I'm a great Jungian. The older I get, the more I rely on my unconscious. I find when I'm writing, these things start coming out, and of course I edit them, so that it's all come out of nowhere. This play I was just writing, I was having to write twelve different kinds of letters. I would just sit down at the typewriter and start to babble in character, so to speak.

**Isn't that a species of automatic writing?**

No, I don't think it's that. With most automatic writing, I think, "Oh for heaven's sake, just chuck it in the wastepaper basket!" Most of the stuff that I have read, there seemed to be no way of getting into it at all. With my own writing, a lot of it is very concrete. For instance, at the beginning of my play an object falls from the sky, and throughout there are twelve different versions of what it was, and they're all Surrealist objects that bear no relation to anything at all. One is a model of the Eiffel Tower made out of toothpicks, one time it's a cast-iron bathtub, another time it's a canoe. I just kind of conjured them up out of my subconscious and put them [in order] of ascending peculiarity. This is obviously a very Surrealist kind of thing, but I tell myself that this isn't absolutely random, because I really worked on it a lot. Of all the things that occurred to me, I polished them, so the play is filled with bizarre, concrete references to objects. I've never tried automatic writing. I think I'd be terrible at it.

**Is pastiche an important part of what you do?**

I tend to think life is pastiche. I'm not sure what it's a pastiche of—we haven't found out yet. I've read an awful lot and looked at an awful lot. I'm a real cultural magpie in that respect. I almost always start as pastiche of some sort. Sometimes it doesn't end up anything like [the source], but you can spot what it's basically doing. It also gives you a framework; that's why I do lots of alphabets, because I can let fly, but there is that basic skeleton there.

**Is there a subversive element in this?**

It depends. Certain things have annoyed me inordinately, and I think, "Someone should really do a number on this." By the time I've gotten around to doing it, I'm actually doing it for its own sake. Whatever anger was in there has gotten submerged, and totally changed from what it started out as.

**I saw some recent reissues at a book fair; you signed them by crossing out your name on the title page.**

Yes. When I was at Harvard in the late 1940s, E. M. Forster delivered a lecture. I dutifully brought up one of my E. M. Forster volumes to be signed. He crossed out his name on the title page and wrote "E. M. Forster." I thought, "This is the way all authors do this." As far as I know, E. M. Forster and myself are the only ones that do.

**What kind of things do you collect?**

Books. I can't go out the door without buying books. I collect art. I collect spherical objects. I collect postcard photographs of dead babies. (Everybody says, *"Don't tell them that."*) I got started accidentally. I had a postcard of a baby which looked like it was asleep, but someone said they thought that baby was dead. I said, "Well, how could it be . . . I mean, uggh!" Now I discover that there are other pictures [like this], not only babies. You know, when travel was difficult, people had gone out to the frontiers and whatnot, people were losing babies right and left. This is at the turn of the century. They would have a baby all dressed up and photographed—sometimes it's sitting up in a chair, sometimes on a little bed, most often in a coffin. The only one that really gets to me a little bit—I've seen reproductions—is a photograph of a youngish family posed with a dead baby in a coffin, which does give pause.

**Does anyone share your collecting interests?**

Not that I know of. I have a friend in New York who has a huge collection of postcards. He goes to these postcard shows and sheepishly says, "Any dead babies?" to the dealers. He tells me, "I hate it!" I say, "Well, just keep looking."

# Writing *The Black Doll*: A Talk with Edward Gorey

Annie Nocenti,

*Scenario*, Spring 1998

A striking figure with a long white beard, [Edward Gorey] speaks in a voice by turns lilting, sigh-laden, passionate and dramatizing, pitching itself up and down, and peppered with sound effects. As he speaks and gestures, his hands chime with little brass creatures that run down every finger, an effect achieved by numerous rings.

**Louis Feuillade,[1] the early 1900s silent-film-maker, seems to be a kindred spirit for you. Was he, in part, the inspiration for *The Black Doll*?**

Yes, I would think. The first Feuillades I saw were the fragments left of *Fantômas*. I saw *Tih-Minh* and *Les Vampires* and *Barrabas*, which I

think is the greatest movie ever made. Unfortunately, I've never seen *Judex*. But on top of my list for movies I'd like to see before I die are any of the Feuillades I haven't seen, and I haven't seen all that many.

**There are seven or eight hundred of them, aren't there?**

But a lot of them are short! The ones I'm curious about are the ones after the serial thrillers. There's one called *The Two Orphans*, which is part thriller and part domestic piece.

**Your simpatico with Feuillade is in the feeling the films evoke, the atmosphere?**

Well, one can't help being swept away by what Paris looked like around World War I. It's footage that said "hello" to me more than anything else I'd ever seen.

The films are cozy, with domestic settings, and they have sinister underpinnings. There's a German word which is the word for cozy but with the negative attached to it,[3] so that it's cozy and sinister, settled and unsettling, cozy and uncozy.

**Those elements are certainly in *The Black Doll*?**

I hope so!

**Doorbells that are never touched, yet ring. Misplaced gloves. Little touches that seep into your unconscious and create a sense of foreboding. You have a cinematic style, like Feuillade, in that you pick shots that culminate to create a feeling.**

Feuillade, in a sense, is very primitive. He'll have three people talking and they're all looking at the camera. Simply because it was easier to do it that way back then. But every now and again there will be some extraordinary bit of business in Feuillade. In one of his films—maybe

*The Danse Macabre*, one of the ones with the black tights and the whole bit—someone has a piece of rope wrapped around their middle. And then they suddenly drop six stories, they just go "zzzzzup!" and take the rope off their middle and go waltzing away! It's so shocking, it's out of nowhere and it only lasts a couple of seconds, but you never forget it.

**And why did you decide to write a screenplay?**

Well, I'm a great one for drift. And so I never met anybody who was involved in movies or anything. But as far as that goes, within about a month of when my first book came out, in 1953, people were saying "Oh, we should make a movie out of this. Oh, we'd love to do an animation." And that's about the end of that. Nothing's ever come of anything.

**Your printed illustrative work uses cinematic perspective—**

Well, I've been watching movies for close to seventy years. My family took me to movies very early. I've always been an inveterate moviegoer. There was a period in New York when I would see a thousand movies a year.

**That's almost three a day!**

I had a friend, Bill Everson, who ran a film series, so he had an incredible collection. He would have these marathon film sessions, twenty-four hours long. In those days I would sit through anything. Someone would get very cross and say, "Really, Bill, why are we sitting through this dreadful movie?" And they wouldn't be invited back for several weeks or months sometimes.

But I would sit through anything. There was this film, about some Finnish girl who had won a Miss Universe contest, and she married a wealthy Philippine businessman, and he decided to make a movie about their lives. The whole first reel was devoted to the credits. She played herself, of course. I can't remember if there were actors or what. It was nine reels. After the first three reels, Bill said, "I'm sorry, I can't watch any more of this." And I said, "Oh, don't you want to know how it comes out?" And about a year later he said, "Let's watch the rest of that thing." Nobody else, of course, would have been caught dead in the same room with it. So we watched three more reels. And again he said, "I can't, I can't, I can't." And I said, "Okay." And then another year or two passed and we finally saw the last three reels, in which they found lasting happiness, of course.

**Why did you decide to write a silent-film script?**

Because I really do think movies made a terrible mistake when they started to talk, for the most part.

**Why did the silent films appeal to you?**

It's what you had to leave out. The greatest single talent the movies ever produced was Charlie Chaplin. Not my favorite—my idol is Buster Keaton.

**Do you like silent films because the imagination is more engaged?**

Yes, because our imagination is engaged, whereas movies today get more in your face by the moment. What has killed movies is the special effects. See one screen filled with flames and you've seen all of them. For instance, now trailers are back in vogue. For years, you never saw a trailer for anything, so you didn't know what the movies were going to be like. But lately, if you go to any action movies, you see trailers for six more action films. They're all the same movie. And if it's a special-effects movie, you've seen all the effects already in the trailer, so don't bother to go.

**What is it that's happening to film language? Are those films afraid of subtlety?**

I don't know, because I think that the other kinds of movies that are portentously not big, the ones that are small, and "period," and . . . well, let me just say that I think Merchant-Ivory has a lot to answer for! They're just so desperately trying not to do anything.

But then, for years, everyone said the studio system was so evil—you know, poor Judy Garland, poor Bette Davis. Obviously, Leonardo DiCaprio is a bigger star than anybody's ever seen before. But now movies sink people sooner or later. They appear on the screen and you think, "Ooo! Goody!" and by the time the movie is over you think, "Oh, God, they just sank without a trace into the end of the movie!" Whereas in the old days, with the star system, people were pushed up out of the movie. It could be a good movie or a bad movie, but it was showing off something. . . .

**An individual talent, something idiosyncratic?**

Yes, like Bette Davis. God knows she was in some real clinkers, but they were always entertaining. When I was growing up, I thought Bette Davis wildly overacted. When she was in a good movie she was faithful to it. She didn't run amok. But when she saw that the movie was just absolutely bad, she would pull out every stop, she would keep you entertained. And even then I don't think she falsified what she was doing.

I remember a film, and in this case I will name names, and that was *Body Heat*. I thought, "If this movie starts over one more time I'm going to leave the theater." As I recollect it, they started the movie the way you start a film noir. In a film noir, in two minutes they've given you all the information you need and then we were off. Instead of this, *Body Heat* started over again, and gave us two more minutes which gave you exactly the same information in a different way. And by about five or six times, I thought, "Oh, please. Get on with the movie." I think they've forgotten how to make a movie. For instance, I thought *L. A. Confidential* was quite the splendid movie, but it was close to thirty minutes too long. It was all very interesting, what was going on in the first part, but you didn't need it. Too much narration, heavy explanations. Endless voice-overs. And I thought, "Why are you telling me all this? What is this blather?"

**Some of your illustrated stories read like silent films. I'm thinking of *The West Wing*. *The Object-Lesson* is masterly in letting the imagination be engaged.**

I always feel, "what you see is what you get," but if you want to read something into it, then you can. Occasionally, someone will come up to me and say, "Oh, I figured out what your book was about." And I say, "Oh, what?" And they'll tell me something completely bizarre. And I'll think, "If that's what you want to see, it's okay by me."

*save for a card on which was written the single word:*

**In your film script, *The Black Doll*, what is "The PRO"?**

It's a "Priceless Ritual Object."

**And you created it to be the thing people chase, like a MacGuffin?[4]**

Yes. You know, it really is amazing that until Mr. Hitchcock pointed it out, no one had really thought about it in exactly those terms. When you stop and think about it, what motivates most thrillers is completely inexplicable. My favorite is, "This treaty, if it isn't recovered, will mean World War III!" And you think, "Huh? What?"

**It's just plot propulsion. Fuel.**

Well, exactly, but not if you stop and think about it. I guess it makes it simple if you just have one particular thing, but I always think, "Why couldn't someone just be called up on the telephone to clear it all up?" My favorite thriller of all time is *The Lady Vanishes*. But you keep thinking, "Why don't you just send a postcard to somebody and fix this?"

*Farewell.*

Ce livre est dédié à Chagrin,
Qui fit un petit mannequin:
  Sans bras et tout noir,
  Il était affreux voir;
En effet, absolument la fin.

**"The PRO," which is inside the Black Doll in the script, is a MacGuffin within a MacGuffin. The Black Doll reappears in several of your stories. Does it have other significance for you?**

A friend of mine made the original Black Doll—which, I believe, I left in a hotel room somewhere. It disappeared sometime in the '40s and it's never been seen again.

**And is it a premonition of tragedy, the Black Doll?**

No, whenever I can't think of anything else to do, I think, "Oh, well, I'll do 'The Return of the Black Doll.' "

**Your book *The Hapless Child* had one that was ripped apart.**

Oh, yes, Charlotte Sophia. It was ripped to pieces, poor dear.[5] I got that from somewhere. Everything I do I get from somewhere; unfortunately, I never remember where. I guess *The Blue Aspic*, my opera book, is filled with all sorts of private jokes. There was one I couldn't even figure out myself when I was reading it again. Then, a few years later, I was reading a book about Fritz Lang and I thought, "Oh, that's where I got this!" Fritz Lang was another of my great influences.

**In *The Blue Aspic*, the opera star rises while another man falls. It has the movement of a dance to it.**

Things get worse and worse for him until finally she gets her comeuppance. I just used an archetypical opera plot.

**You've been very influenced by the ballet also, and at one point in *The Black Doll* there is an ensemble balletic dance at the masquerade ball. Everyone is spinning around so much that one of the characters gets giddy.**

Well, I spent an awfully long time watching ballet, and I tend to draw people in vaguely balletic postures. When you're doing stories that are as short as mine are, the less realistic they are, the better. It's almost impossible to be realistic, so anything that is stylized is good. I've done a lot of theater, and I'm not at all interested in realistic theater. It's always very stylized.

Years ago someone did a revue of a bunch of my work on Broadway, called *Gorey Stories*. It was one of those legendary things that opened and closed on the same night. My name was in lights, but not very big ones.

Anyway, I started putting on plays of my own books. They're not like revues because they don't start and stop, they just sort of drivel along without interruption. I've got a lot of manuscripts I've never illustrated, so I do those, and I always direct myself. I pick something, and I think, "Well, there's no way of putting this on stage." And then I think, "Oh, sure there is!" The past few years I've been writing more for the stage. Very stylized. I use the same local actors. Most of them aren't professional in that they don't make their living as actors, but I have an incredibly talented group I work with.

I always do goofy casting. For instance, when we did *The Gilded Bat*, which is my ballet piece, I had Maudie Splaytoe, the ballerina, played by a young black man who was six-foot-four. He was absolutely hilarious.

**Are your characters archetypes that anyone can play?**

Yes. For instance, one of my actors is in his late forties. He gets heavier every year and has a full, bushy beard. Once, I don't know why, I cast him in a heart-rending little work about a mother whose child is eaten by a pack of wild dogs. It was a little anecdote someone told me, they swore it was true.

He played the mother, and she has this little girl about two or three years old. She keeps buying her little girl clothes made of bunny fur—first the hat, then a coat, then leggings, then boots and little mittens, until she has a complete set. She inadvertently leaves her child outside of the greengrocer while she's inside buying eggplants, and a pack of wild dogs comes by and tears this child in bunny fur to pieces!

**In terms of all the mysterious machinations in *The Black Doll*, were you influenced at all by the Charlie Chan or Fu Manchu movies?**[6]

Fu Manchu, Charlie Chan, *The Perils of Pauline*.[7] One great influence on me, in an idiotic way, was a film that no one ever put together. The Museum of Modern Art just had all the footage of it. It was Italian, a serial, called *Grey Rats*. But it was completely out of context. You'd be watching and say, "Oh, this happened half an hour ago." Somebody had thrown it all together in a big box, on reels, and we watched it that way. It took about two weeks.

**Do you find the mysterious, or rather the structure of mystery, to be a good structure to use in your stories, for the feeling you try to evoke?**

Yes. I've read mystery stories all my life. I've read everything Agatha Christie's written about five times. People say, "Oh, mysteries. You can only read them once." But I don't think that's true at all.

I've always been interested in True Crime. Now True Crime makes me want to throw up, but I'm talking about the days when people murdered just one person in the household, and that was it, folks. We didn't run amok with serial killers and so forth. The worst thing going was Jack the Ripper. But in reading accounts of True Crime, you learn all sorts of things about how people live. Nothing particularly outrageous, but strange and interesting. Anyone's life is—I mean, look at mine!

**Getting back to *The Black Doll*—**

Well, *The Black Doll* was very much inspired by so many of the D. W. Griffiths[8] that were made out in New Jersey. One of the great things about those early movies is that you get to see what everything looked like then. Like California in the early days, those wonderful backgrounds for comedies, a strange little bungalow sitting out in the middle of nowhere, streetcars going by . . .

**The empty streets, the anonymous humans—**

The empty street, yes, and there was something about photography in those days. If *The Black Doll* were ever to be made, I mean obviously he's dead, but there was a French cameraman named Eugen Schüftan who was over here working who would have been perfect. My favorite horror movie is Franju's *Eyes Without a Face*. That was photographed by Schüftan.[9]

**Georges Franju? He did a remake of Feuillade's *Judex*.**

That's one of my favorite movies. I adore the whole movie, but the masquerade ball in Franju's *Judex*, with everyone wearing bird masks, is an homage to Feuillade and I think it's absolutely brilliant. And the business with the two ladies, one in black, one in white, fighting on the rooftop—that whole scene is very Feuillade—also where everyone in black is climbing up the side of the building.

**I didn't expect gadgetry in Franju's *Judex*, such as the surveillance camera. Did Feuillade use gadgetry?**

Not that I know of. But most of those Feuillades weren't really serials. They were chapters in a sequence. They would go out and shoot in the streets of Paris, which is what gives them that wonderful look. In the middle of *Les Vampires*, some actor kept arriving on the set late, so they just fired him. So he disappears after chapter five or six, and somebody else comes in, an entirely different person.

The Surrealists loved Feuillade, loved how he kept resurrecting evil end-lessly. But later on, some historian revealed that Feuillade had to fire actors and replace them, and that's what the resurrections were about.

Yes, utterly pragmatic reasons.

He used cheaply constructed sets, and everyone praised him at the time for his use of realism. But again, some historian figured out that he was simply short of funds, and came up with the "realism" rhetoric to cover for it. He also had trouble with censorship in his time, for his anti-heroes, and for his glorification of villainy.

Oh, did he?

In *The Black Doll*, there's a curious element to the Asiatics—we, the viewer, see them, but the characters don't.

There's a movie I'm dying to see again—[Jacques Tourneur's] *The Curse of the Demon*. It's a great horror movie, from a story by M. R. James,[10] who does very cozy but very scary ghost stories, which I do not read before I go to bed. It was a marvelous low-budget movie, and in it was a children's party, where a sinister magician is the villain of the piece. The camera shifts a viewpoint—you expect to see somebody there but they're not there. This is repeated once or twice. It gives you a great sense of unease, without your being able to say exactly why.

So with your unseen Asiatics, and also the multiple Joshuas—one actor playing multiple roles—you also create a sense of unease.

I rather like the idea of that kind of manipulation of things. It calls attention to, I'm not sure what—

That we should suspect everyone?

In those old movies, I think sometimes people did play two or three roles just by changing costume or putting on a mustache. The whole idea of disguise. Like in those Elizabethan plays where no one seems to recognize anybody despite the fact that they've been living together for a hundred years. Or the bed trick. Someone wrote a thesis on the bed trick in Elizabethan drama. You know, when the maid becomes the mistress and the husband never realizes it even though they've been sleeping together forever. It's one of those wonderful loopy conventions. What's that later Buñuel film—

*That Obscure Object of Desire?* **Where he casts two women in the same role?**[11]

Right. Yes. Talk about loopy!

**He claimed it happened during casting, that he simply couldn't make up his mind between the two actresses.**

One of the wonderful things about Buñuel was his marvelous loony quality, in which he puts things into his movies that I'm sure he didn't sit there thinking out. I remember one of his Mexican films, where this man falls in love with a totally inaccessible woman, maybe it's in *The Criminal Life of Archibaldo de La Cruz.* Anyway, at one point, he has a wax dummy made of her, which he puts into a pottery kiln, and he gleefully watches her melt away. The film was filled with all sorts of faintly bizarre instruments of torture—and it was a funny, light-hearted movie.

**As in *Un Chien Andalou,* it may have been from the Surrealist notion of letting the symbols of your unconscious come out unexplained, which I think you do, also, in your work.**

I never find myself having to think up anything, so to speak. I vaguely feel that one thing will do as well as another. I think Flaubert has a lot to answer for. He'd spend days writing a single sentence, anguishing over this or that. I think possibly the dullest novel ever written was

*Salammbô*. He must have read hundreds of books on ancient Carthage, and it's filled with endless details, and I think, "Oh, God, what bother." On the other hand, I think *Sentimental Education* is probably the great French novel of the 19th century, so there you are.

**There is a great Alain Resnais[12] quote: "Feuillade's cinema is very close to dreams; therefore it's perhaps the most realistic."**

Resnais, at one point, was going to remake *Fantômas*, and he did a book of photographs of locations that he might use, of the old Paris, which were dazzling.

**I brought a film to show you, *Irma Vep*, by Olivier Assayas, about a French director who wants to pay homage to Feuillade. Maggie Cheung plays Irma Vep, and gets into this skintight black catwoman outfit. The director has her creep around, exactly as Feuillade did. So after the rushes, the filmmaker has a revelation that he's turned Irma Vep into an object, a fetish, and his big flaw in trying to re-create Feuillade was that he never should have violated the depth-of-field that Feuillade used. He realized that once he altered that cinematic perspective, it fell apart.**

Oh, yes. That's interesting, because in Feuillade's films, I never think of close-ups, and everything is a certain way. In *Fantômas*, there's a moment when Juve arrests Fantômas in a supper club, and he's wearing a cape, or rather one of those capecoats, with holes for the arms, and Juve and Fandor grab Fantômas and take him out into the street. Suddenly, Fantômas just steps out and runs away down the street—the arms turn out to be fake! It's a wonderful dislocation of reality. Here they are holding his arms, taking him off to the pokey, and poof! It's preposterous, and one of the great moments.

Once, they follow Fantômas to a water tank—it's huge, almost to the ceiling. They climb up and peer into the tank and it's full of water, so they go on. And the camera pans back and there's just a straw sticking out of the water—you know he's down there in the water. They're very simple films.

**All Feuillade's characters are such fun. He was right on the pulse of new inventions in character, what with his femmes fatales, his bungling detectives—**

Yes. My idea of heaven would be to have every single film Feuillade ever made and be able to run them off. *Barrabas*, which I only saw once, was the best movie I ever saw. Part of it takes place before World War I and part of it after. I remember two elderly men talking in a rose garden. I remember thinking this was the best thing I'd ever seen, and the only thing that really explained to me what it was like to live before World War I, and how it changed, living after World War I. The film is about a secret society, everyone has this wonderful tattoo, and I think Feuillade invented that kind of thing. It was the first time I ever saw that kind of thing in a film.

**My favorite scene in *The Black Doll* is the way you end it, or rather, the way you evoke a sense of ending with a series of shots—a postcard is torn up, someone wipes a word away, a blind is drawn, a wind comes up, a trunk lid shuts, leaves blow, the doll falls . . .**

Oh yes, all those shots, and a shot of the Fiend as a wax dummy. I always saw Donald Pleasence as the Fiend. I had people in mind for various characters.

I think the hardest kind of movie to make is one that doesn't call any attention to the acting, or the decor, or the music—that's one of my pet peeves now; it seems that every movie I see now is music wall-to-wall. One of the things I most admire about Clouzot[13] is that he never had any music in the main part of his films. Well, the very end of *Diabolique*, that last shot, some music comes up. That is one of the truly great films.

There's this one Clouzot, one of the greatest goofy movies ever made, called *La Prisonnière*. I think it was the only movie he ever made in color. It all takes place in a kind of arty milieu, so that the color is very Mondrian—dead white and then bright blue, bright red, bright yellow, and black. It had one sequence that I thought was mesmerizing as a piece of unobtrusive surrealism. There's a scene where two men are confronting each other on typical Parisian roofs, about six or eight stories above the street. When you first see them confronting each other, all the awnings on the windows are blood red, and one or two awnings are down. With each succeeding shot, more awnings are down, so by the end of the scene the whole place is drenched in red awnings. There's no explanation, it's quite impossible, and wonderfully hair-raising. I don't remember him doing anything else quite so gratuitous, so to speak. Things like that, the movies can do what no one else can do. I suppose in a way you could count those red awnings as a special effect.

Oh well. I told you I used to go to a thousand movies a year, and now I go to hardly any.

**Who would you think of to direct *The Black Doll*?**

Werner Herzog. Although I don't think his sense of humor is exactly there. Lars von Trier. I love him. And there is one French director, Francis Girod. He did *The Infernal Trio*,[14] which is one of the greatest dippy movies ever made. It was based on a real case, about two sisters and a man, all of whom are sociopathic. They would alternate this plan—for instance, he would marry an elderly woman and they would take out insurance and she would expire, and then one of the girls would marry someone, and so forth. It's hilarious. It's a beautifully photographed period piece, very elegant, and yet loopy. I can't remember how it ends, probably badly.

There's another French director, Jean-Pierre Mocky.[15] He made a film about somebody stealing from poorboxes in churches, and another one in a dairy—I remember someone being pushed into a vat of milk. He could do *The Black Doll*.

I love Stephan Elliott, who did *The Adventures of Priscilla, Queen of the Desert*. He made another film about an insurance scam, with Phil Collins as the insurance agent who lives in a fancy house filled with mechanical toys. A very odd movie and quite brilliant. And then there's Pedro Almodóvar. He made a wonderful film about a woman who sells her little boy to a dentist. Her husband has left her and life is difficult, and the dentist likes her little boy, so she sells him to the dentist, and everyone lives happily ever after. It's all very bright and vinyl, with tacky decor, crepe paper and God knows what—it had a great throwaway quality to it.

**So someone from a far-flung country to direct *The Black Doll*. Who would risk a silent movie now?**

Nobody. Except as a novelty.

# The Connection

Christopher Lydon,

*WBUR, Boston, National Public Radio,*

November 26, 1998

Ted Gorey, it's very nice to be here. Do you do Thanksgiving yourself? Are you a holiday person?

No, I hate holidays.

**Why?**

I mean, you know, I think Christmas is really a family holiday. My best Christmases were when I was in New York, and I hung around with a lot of people who also didn't have any families or anything. We used to go to four or five movies on Christmas Day. We'd have breakfast at Howard Johnson's, and then we'd go to a movie—and then we'd go back to the Howard Johnson's. Then we'd go to another movie, and go back to Howard Johnson's—'til about midnight.

**So what does Edward Gorey do for Thanksgiving?**

Thanksgiving I do absolutely nothing. Well, actually, I have cousins down here, so I end up going to them for Thanksgiving.

**Address the legend of Edward Gorey, starting with the fact that you read everything.**

I mean, it's just that I've read so much that nobody else has read. I mean, you know, you can find whole incredible areas. . . . I don't know a thing about American literature at this point—I mean contemporary American literature. I barely recognize the names. I used to keep up with English literature, but now I don't even know who those people are, with one or two exceptions.

**Do you re-read?**

Actually, at the moment I'm re-reading all of Sherlock Holmes, for no particular reason. Some stuff I no longer re-read, because I practically—I mean, you know, I found myself mumbling along with it. And I feel, "Well, much as I'd like to re-read this, there isn't much point."

**What's the part you know practically by heart?**

Oh, I know Jane Austen pretty much by heart. I know the Lucia books by E. F. Benson by heart. I would know *The Tale of Genji* by heart if I understood it better. I haven't re-read that much of Trollope. I mean, I've re-read Trollope, to a certain extent. But, actually, I find that when I pick one up I know it as if I had re-read it. On the other hand, I just re-read *The Man Without Qualities*[1] for the third or fourth time. I didn't remember a word. Of course, I've never understood it. . . .

**Go back to the legend. Edward Gorey is supposed to know everything about Japanese literature, but also about *As the World Turns* and the afternoon soaps.**

I haven't watched the afternoon soaps for a while. I'll do it religiously for about six months—you know, one or two of them—and then I think, "I really can't stand these people another minute!" And so I stop. And then, occasionally, I'll surf and see if something is beginning to intrigue me, and then I'll watch it for a while. But I think TV is getting worse and worse. Most of the new shows I think, "What did anybody think they were doing?" I'm living for the last year of *The X-Files* to come back. I can hardly wait.

**What is your mind and your imagination doing when you watch that stuff?**

Oh, just having a good time. And I'm very fond of *Buffy the Vampire Slayer*. I recommend that highly to everybody.

**Does high-culture Gorey meet low-culture Gorey and say hello from time to time? Or is it all one spectrum, or what?**

It depends on how tired I am. Or if I'm not working terribly hard myself, I can do more high culture than I would—I mean that's why I'm re-reading Sherlock Holmes. It's not because I've got so much to do and stuff. I still have my little high-culture pursuits, every now and again.

**What's the connection between Gorey input and Gorey output?**

Oh, I don't know. The longer I go on, the more I'm just grabbing at whatever happens to be around and hoping, you know, you can fit it in somewhere. Well, mostly I've been doing theater lately and it gets more and more addled. I'm not really sure. There obviously is input and output, but some of it will be input from thirty years ago and some of it will be something I saw just yesterday.

*They visited the ruins of the Crampton vinegar works, which had been destroyed by a mysterious explosion the preceding fall.*

**You were famous in the Broadway stage for your work with *Dracula*—on the designs and the costumes. Was that the bug that got you into the theater, in general?**

Well, I think, in a kind of way, it's been theater all along, except nobody ever asked me to do anything. And about the time of *Dracula* there was this little work called *Gorey Stories*, which somebody from the University of Kentucky put together and it managed, by the skin of its teeth, to get on Broadway for a couple of weeks—and then it officially opened and closed on the same night.

**Are you devoting a lot of your productive time, working time, now to theater?**

Quite a lot. Because I always think, "Oh well, I'll write the play and then we'll have the rehearsals and everything." But, of course, when I'm in six weeks of rehearsal, and, you know, like three weeks of production, I don't do a thing the other part of the day.

**But you haven't explained: What is the lure of the theater for you? What is it you want to say?**

Well, I think it's partly because it's so interesting, not only finding out what you have said—which, you know, is neither here nor there—but just watching something come out that you don't really know what it is to begin with.

**For example.**

Well—oh dear. Well, this was a bad experiment, what I did this summer. A couple of the actors I work with did readings of *Love Letters* to raise money, and so forth, and so on.

**This is A. R. Gurney?**

Yes. And I thought that the play would drive me absolutely up the wall within two minutes. But I thought, "How fiendishly clever. Every overage actor and actress—you know." And I believe that his directions are that you can only read it through once before you go on with it. And you can't have a set. And you have to read it—you can't memorize it. So, of course, you can do it anywhere, at any time. And I thought, "I'm going to sit down and write a play for two people, that is read."

Well, needless to remark, it ran totally and completely amok. It doesn't have two characters; it has sixteen characters. Four of whom do not write letters to each other, but the others—there are six pairs of people who write letters to each other and they're divided as to sex, and age, and everything else.

Partly we did it because I only had three of my regular actors. So what I decided to do was to have A and B, and then you can have B read A and A read B. So that's two. And then you can have A and C, and C and A, and you can have B and C and C and B. So you have six different performances with just three people. We didn't have enough rehearsal. Nobody thought they needed rehearsal. And there was the whole problem of what is the other person doing while somebody else is reading?

**This is news to a lot of people that are going to be doing Edward Gorey two-man, four-man, eight-man plays around the world one of these days.**

Well, if I can get anybody to do it.

**What's the spirit of this epistolary drama?**

Well, it has an insanely complicated plot. It's kind of an English country-house thing, and I'm trying to remember. There are two children who are cousins. She's a year or two older than he is, and they both go to private school. His mother is her father's sister. And then they have a grandfather who doesn't appear—and there are two main houses. There's a couple who are engaged, who never—who are completely uninvolved with everybody else, but all they talk about are the wedding presents they've received. And then there are a pair of villains, like Boris and Natasha from *Bullwinkle*.

**Do they speak in rhyming couplets?**

No, no. No, they speak ordinarily and everything. And then there are four houseguests who write to other people, telling them what's going on and everything. There's this incredibly complicated plot, which gets absolutely nowhere. And the thing is, everybody comes up to me afterward and says, "Oh, do you have a copy of the script I can read?" Meaning, of course, "I couldn't follow this! I'm exhausted!"

**But this is wonderfully like the way people read your books—the way I've been reading your books for thirty-five years. I think I started with *The Doubtful Guest* in the, what, the mid-60s? A gift from my sister. And I've probably read it fifty times since then, and I laugh all the way. I'm not sure what you meant or why I like it. Do you watch children today? Are you close to children?**

Oh, heavens, no. I don't think I know a single child. Do I know a single child?

**Have you ever changed a diaper?**

Oh, God, no—no. No. And, actually, all my friends' children were grown up and in college. I can't imagine what it would be like to be a child today. Poor little things glued to the television set. The one thing that really does rather baffle me—I go yard-sale-ing every Saturday— and last week it seemed to be mostly young couples having yard sales.

And then, of course, other young people are coming in. There were maybe two or three or maybe four small children around and everything. They were getting rid of enormous cartons of stuff. Well, they were getting rid of clothes, too. But enormous cartons of stuffed animal after stuffed animal after stuffed animal. Every child, I feel, on Cape Cod must have about fifty stuffed animals! And, usually, some of them are totally un—even looked at.

Well, of course, look at after Princess Di died. I mean, everybody's sending teddy bears now. It's the great symbol of: "We care." Though I did wonder, with Diana, if it went from stuffed animals to real animals? Perhaps living, perhaps dead? Did it ever get badly enough off so that somebody abandoned a live baby amidst all the flowers? Or even a dead one?

**Ooooh.**

I wouldn't be a bit surprised if there weren't some very peculiar things left in those heaps.

**What is the world of childhood in Edward Goreyana? And what does Edward Gorey's childhood have to do with it, if anything?**

Not a great deal, I don't suppose. For some reason or other, I was trying to remember my bedroom in my high-school days—and already it was filled with books. Not that any of these things were assigned reading, as far as I know. But when I look back now, there was all the Evelyn Waugh to date, and all of Aldous Huxley. Well, my family was very big on detective stories. I mean, we all read Agatha Christie. You know, Ngaio Marsh, Margery Allingham, Dorothy Sayers, and so forth and so on. One of my mother's sisters was very big on Jane Austen. So I read Jane Austen very early and she became my favorite author. I didn't start reading Dickens until I was in college, I don't think. Though we did have a wonderful horrid thing called *Child Stories from Dickens*. It was all the deaths. Little Nell. What's his name from *Nicholas Nickleby*?

**Smike.**

I remember it with horror.

**That inspired the long alphabet of kids dying, one way or another?**

Oh, I don't know—it probably just came to me. My better works just came to me, I think. I think if you have to think about anything very long, you've obviously done yourself an injury, as it were.

**Does anybody else out there do what you do? Or are you a category of one?**

I think I'm a category of one. Which has its advantages and disadvantages, I think. There are people I admire enormously, that I don't feel I really, you know, could possibly, you know, get anything from, so to speak. Though I keep trying. Well, I mean, the greatest influence on me probably is George Balanchine—and don't ask me why. I'm not really sure. But I got more from him. Everything he ever said about art, in the larger sense, was only too true.

**You don't mean from conversations. You mean from watching his . . .**

Oh, no, no. I'd been introduced to him once or twice. I found him very off-putting. Partly, you know—

**I don't know, but go ahead.**

Well, for one thing, his English was not great. There was no impulse to get chummy with him. You know, I think the only people who were really chummy with him, apart from some of the dancers, were his old friends from Russia. But, as I say, I think, from not exactly a technical point of view, but from everything he said about art and the way he put ballets together, I think, you know, he was the one authentic genius that I ever—

**What did he teach you? I mean, if there's a way to paraphrase it.**

Well, I really don't know. Whatever he said about ballet was really applicable to practically everything else. Not that he was trying to be, or anything. Well, I think one thing he taught me, above all, is "don't waffle." I mean, he was just as liable to say, "Well, I wouldn't do that," to some dancer. "Better don't do" was one of his phrases. Or, on the other hand, "Just do it!" You know, don't dither.

I think the fact that he always said, "Just do the steps". . . You know, he had all sorts of dancers, and some of them were overly intellectual. And you could see their tiny little minds seething away: "What does all this mean, when I do this?" Or "What's my motivation for lifting my leg?" So you'll be up in arabesque—that's your motivation for lifting your leg. Or you won't be in arabesque. So his best dancers, I think, just did it. And he knew enough about their personalities and what they could do, so that fairly soon, really, in the proceedings, you know, they would come up with what—

**How does a writer-illustrator apply that?**

Well, I try not to presuppose what I'm doing. I just do it. And I think, "Oh, dear, this drawing doesn't work. Hell, I'll have to do it over again." Which doesn't happen often. I mean, I usually desperately try and retrieve it. But I usually don't know what I've done until long after I've done it. Since I very seldom look at a book after it's done, it may be years before I have some reason to look at it and see what I think it was about. Maybe it wasn't about that at all.

**Does the Gorey World have anything to do with reality? Or is it all about artifice and surrealism?**

I think it's got a lot to do with reality. I think my stuff is really quite real. I mean, people endlessly nattering about nothing at all. Terrible things happening or nothing happening. You know, I'm not a firm believer in cause and effect.

**What about reality and fantasy? Where do you live?**

Oh, you know, "fantasy" I've always found a word I really don't care for. Fantasy always strikes me as something that doesn't have any reality because it's completely irresponsible. Anything that is just fantastic I don't think is really terribly interesting.

What's the Coleridge distinction between imagination and—is it fantasy? I don't think that's the word. Anyway, you know, one is meaningful and one isn't. Not that I'm trying to be meaningful, exactly. I don't know.

**What's the connection between fantasy and nonsense? Are you happier thinking of living in a nonsense world?**

Oh, dear. There's a book by Elizabeth Sewell,[2] which was the best book on nonsense I've ever read. It was mostly about Lewis Carroll and Edward Lear. *Alice* and Lear's limericks and everything are nonsense, but they have a connection with sense. Whereas fantasy seems to be totally arbitrary at its worst. You know, you just think up something odd. Or you can start with the endless numbers of children's books which are stuck together with the first rhyme that comes into somebody's head for an animal's name or something. Well, I don't wish to denigrate Dr. Seuss, but I mean, you know, "the cat in the hat."

But [what I'm doing] always seems quite meaningful at the time. Maybe it's because it's going through my mind with the speed of light.

But it does occur to me that, you know, you don't necessarily have to think in words or that, at least, they can be very subliminal. I think my mind gets more in the way than it used to. I think I used to just write things and that was it. Now I know it gets in the way of my drawing. I find myself thinking, "Now, you know, what's the content of this drawing? And should I do it this way or that?" And I think, "I didn't used to be this way—I'd just sit down and do the damn thing."

# Playing Favorites

Kerry Fried,

*Amazon.com,* November 1998

We asked some of our favorite authors for a few words (if not paragraphs) on the book or books they most admired or adored in 1998. In the spirit of the season, several went beyond the bounds of brevity—and did so with our enthusiastic blessing. Many thanks to all who took part in this annual, deeply unscientific census.—Kerry Fried.

Edward Gorey: "I am almost never invited to tell the world at large what it ought to be reading. Thank you for the opportunity.

"First, *Exercises in Style* by Raymond Queneau, for me the reference book for creative inspiration. I am forever dipping into it, if not reading it cover to cover, which takes less than an hour. Thirteen novels by Queneau are available in English translation; each is different from the others, but they are all delightful—read every one.[1]

"Second, the five Mennyms books by Sylvia Waugh.[2] This domestic saga is published as being for children so that most adults are unlikely to find it except by accident, which is a great pity. In their strangeness they bring to mind the fiction of such authors as say, Charles Williams and E. W. H. Meyerstein;[3] otherwise they are unlike anything but themselves.

"Third, Robert Musil's *The Man Without Qualities*—The Great Modern Novel, or whatever. Very long, difficult, and far from finished, all of it, including lots of fragments, is for the first time available in English translation. Also a massive selection of his diaries, although only about two-fifths of the German original, has just appeared. I look forward to another lengthy, strenuous, but exhilarating read."[4]

# Edward Gorey's Cover Story

Steven Heller,

*The National Post* (Toronto), Wednesday, January 6, 1999

I n 1953 [Edward Gorey] published his first book, *The Unstrung Harp*, a wry tale illustrated in a satiric Edwardian style, about the trials and tribulation of the author C. F. Earbrass. The same year he accepted a job in the art department of Anchor/Doubleday, where he did paste-ups, lettering, and designed about fifty book covers (he left in 1960). These illustrated covers comprise a small but significant chapter in the history of paperback cover design and the legacy of the bearded, fur-coated spectre who made them. In this interview, Edward Gorey recalls these now forgotten (but not lost) artifacts.

**How did you become a book cover designer of Anchor/Doubleday?**

I knew editors Barbara Zimmerman and Jason Epstein from my days at Harvard, and both of them were working at Doubleday. I visited New York just before Christmas 1952, when they were starting Anchor Books; I did some freelance covers for them. Then they offered me a job, which at first I turned down because I didn't want to live in New York. So much for that. I realized that I was starving to death in Boston, and took the job in 1953.

**Why did you go to Harvard?**

I came from Chicago originally and graduated from high school in 1942. I applied to the University of Chicago, Carnegie Tech (as it was known in those days), and Harvard—God knows why. But I went to this kind of fancy, intellectually (so to speak) reputable private school in Chicago, so in those days it was fairly easy to be admitted to Harvard. I couldn't get in now if I crawled on my hands and knees from here to Cambridge. But it was fairly easy if you were fairly bright, and I was fairly bright. So after I got out of the Army in January of 1946, I got a postcard from Harvard—two postcards attached, and you sent back the other one. It said "When are you coming?" I wasn't even thinking about it at the time. However, the G.I. Bill paid my tuition. So I trotted off to Harvard to major in French, without bothering to discover whether they had a particularly good French Department or not. I majored in French and read French literature. So now, every five years I look at my shelves of French books and think, "I really must read something," and so I read four or five books in French and that does that for the next five years.

**Had you any kind of graphic design experience before Harvard?**

No.

**Were you drawing pictures at that time?**

I was drawing, if that's what you want to call it.

**With the intention of becoming . . .**

With the intention of nothing at all, I assure you. I've never had any intentions about anything. That's why I am where I am today, which is neither here nor there, in a literal sense.

**Just a legend in your time.**

Right.

**Were you the art director of Anchor/Doubleday?**

No, I took a job in the art department, mostly doing paste-ups. It wasn't too difficult really. In fact, when I saw some of the paste-ups that other people did, I thought, "They really are all thumbs, these well-known artists." I never had much patience with having to re-do other people's paste-ups, which looked like they'd just flung the letters on the page.

**You did, however, graduate from this menial work to cover design. What was the first book cover that you illustrated and designed on your own?**

There was *Lafcadio's Adventures* by André Gide; next there was a kind of tacky little drawing of the Globe Theatre from the air, which I found someplace and copied for a book on Shakespeare by Mark van Doren. I can't remember what the third one was. They used to go in threes.

**In addition to the drawing style, the most distinctive aspect of your covers was your hand-lettering, which approximated real type. At that time there was a predominance of ornate calligraphy on book covers. Why did you go into the particular direction of faux-type?**

I was stuck with hand-lettering, which I did very poorly, I always felt, but everybody seemed to like it. So I got stuck with it for the rest of my life.

**By that I presume you mean using it in your own subsequent books. But what was the reason you got stuck with it?**

Because when I started publishing my own work everybody said, "Oh, you've got to hand-letter." My first book was not hand-lettered, but my second one was, and after that there was no looking back.

**But this style began with your book covers?**

Most of them were hand-lettered.

**Was type too expensive, was this a financial issue?**

No. I didn't really know too much about type in those days, and it was simply easier to hand-letter the whole thing than to spec type. Eventually I did a lot of things that weren't hand-lettered, as far as bookjackets were concerned.

**Did you read a lot as preparation for illustrating covers?**

Oh, not necessarily. I was usually handed the assignment, and there would be some little paragraph summarizing the plot. Some of the stuff, of course, I'd read.

**But your love of literature, especially French literature, didn't hurt your bookjacket career.**

Oh, no. I was much better-read than most of the people who were doing artwork. I probably still am. I mean, I'm an inveterate reader.

**At the time you were doing covers, was there anybody else in the jacket and cover world that you were looking at for inspiration?**

Probably my admirations in those days were British.

**Is that when you developed your penchant for the Edwardian style that characterizes your own work?**

No, I had a penchant for the British long before that. I was aware of British bookjackets because I bought a lot of British books at the time.

**Speaking of style, did you find that after a while you were self-consciously working in that style, or did it naturally develop?**

There were certain kinds of books where I followed a routine, such as my famous landscape which was mostly sky so I could fit in a title. Things like *The American Tourist* or whatever it was called; *Victory* and *The Wanderer*[1] tend to have low-lying landscapes, a lot of sky, sort of odd colors, and tiny figures that I didn't have to draw very hard.

**That is the very format used for Lermontov's *A Hero of Our Time*.[2] You have two horses and a little. . .**

Doesn't it have a sort of pale green sky?

**A pale green sky, yes, against a pink mountain.**

Right. Well, I assure you that was taken from some painting, maybe by Lermontov himself.

**Since your books are black and white, I am really taken by your color sense for these book covers. They are always muted, very earthy and distinctly subtle.**

Well, it was partly because you had to keep to three flat colors, plus black. I guess I could have picked bright reds or blues, but I've never been much for that. My palette seems to be sort of lavender, lemon-yellow, olive-green, and then a whole series of absolutely no colors at all.

**One of the "no-color" covers which is just gorgeous (and a terrific interpretation) is your cover for Kafka's *Amerika*.**

Oh, yes. That has little pink clouds and not much else. I'm also rather fond of the *Arabia Deserta*[3] which is in three different shades of blah grey-olive.

**For someone who didn't know where he was heading professionally, these covers have a skillful, and unique, sense of composition. Moreover, the characterizations are delightful. You created a very discernible style for the Anchor/Doubleday list.**

It's all a mistake, I assure you. Incidentally, I also became very well known for my covers for Henry James, whom I hate more than anyone else in the world except for Picasso.

**You hate James? Why is that?**

I don't know. I've read everything of Henry James, some of it twice, and every time I do it I think, "Why am I doing this again? Why am I torturing myself? I know how I feel. Why can't I just accept that?"

**But your covers for James are fairly astute interpretations . . .**

Well, everybody thought, "Oh, how sensitive you are to Henry James," and I thought, "Oh sure, kids." If it's because I hate him so much, that's probably true.

**Why did you leave Anchor/Doubleday?**

Jason Epstein had started something called Looking Glass Library with Celia Carroll, and I joined them. The idea was that it was going to do for children's books what Anchor had done for the parents. The books were not paperbacks, but rather paper over boards. And it was really quite a good series. Well, the paper was perfectly dreadful, but then the paper for everything in those days was perfectly terrible.

**What did you do at Looking Glass Library?**

I illustrated a few books (the less said about those, the better), and I was the art director. I also was an editor, in a sense, because I helped pick some of the books. We did at least three of the Andrew Lang colored Fairy Books.[4] We did a few anthologies, including a wonderful anthology of poetry for children by Janet Adams Smith, which started out at Faber in London. Somebody edited something called *The Comic Looking Glass.* I remember I illustrated H. G. Wells' *The War of the Worlds.* Richard Hughes did a wonderful book of children's stories called *The Spider's Palace.* We did Charlotte M. Young's *Countess Kade.* It was really a neat batch of sometimes quite forgotten 19th-century stories. We tended to pick up stuff from England. It was really a good idea, but then Jason lost interest, and after two years the whole thing folded up.

**So after Looking Glass fizzled, what did you do?**

I'd done some work for Vintage [paperback books] off and on. And for a year [1963] I was the art director at Bobbs Merrill, which we all referred to as Boobs Muddle. Eventually there was internecine warfare, and I was unfortunately on the side of the president, who got fired with all his entourage. Which was just as well. After that I just had too much freelance work to look for another job, and I moved up to the Cape.

**I had heard a story that when you were at Anchor/Doubleday you were rummaging through the storeroom and found the original illustrations by George Herriman of the classic book *archy and mehitabel*.[5] Is this true?**

I could scream now, because nobody knew they were there, and I anguished but finally took three of them. We were cleaning out these bins that hadn't been opened since the '20s or '30s, and I thought, "Well, I really shouldn't take the whole book." And I have a feeling that probably the rest of them did get thrown away. Because the Graham Gallery [in New York] used to have shows of Herriman and as far as I know, none of those drawings have ever surfaced since.

**Do you still have those drawings?**

I have this awful feeling that I have the only three originals left. You can't believe how much stuff there was . . . you know, old bookjackets from the '20s, the 'teens. Nobody paid any attention to it.

**I presume that you were a Herriman aficionado. So, who else has excited you over these many years?**

I've been a fan of *Krazy Kat* and I've been excited by so much over the last seventy years that I don't know any more. I sit around looking, and I'm always becoming engrossed and saying, "Gee, I didn't know I knew about this; here it all is."

**When did you stop doing the book cover work?**

Oh, I still do bookjacket work occasionally, if somebody calls me up.

# Miscellaneous Quotes

"Sometimes I think my life would have been completely different if I had ever learned to draw."

**to L. S. "Edward Gorey's Danse Macabre,"** *Los Angeles Times*, **March 2, 1986**

"I think of my books as Victorian novels all scrunched up."

**to Mary Rourke, "Strange Things Happen When Gorey Is Afoot,"** *The National Observer*, **September 11, 1976**

"I really do use reptiles a lot, and I really don't know why. I am rather fond of toads and frogs, lizards, or snakes. Not that I keep any. I've always been partial to dinosaurs."

Is that because they're removed from humanity?

"I suppose there is something to that. Few people seem to notice that a largish part of my stuff is not about human beings. I mean, I've done several books about inanimate objects. But as far as the animals, I just don't think humanity is the ultimate end. We're so smug about ourselves, secure about how much we know. Well, I've lived with cats most of my life, so I'm very aware that there's another world going on. It's sometimes sitting in your lap, so obviously it's not completely different. But it sees everything differently, hears everything differently, and probably thinks differently."

**to Ted Drozdowski, "The Welcome Guest,"** *Boston Phoenix*, **August 21, 1992**

Gorey has ice-blue eyes that don't seem to linger on any object more than a fraction of a second—except on Marianne Moore, the ten-week-old Gotham [Book Mart] resident kitten, whose tininess and light molasses coloring would win the heart of any non-cat person. She certainly has captured Gorey's heart (he is a cat person), and he proudly introduces her to a friend who stops by briefly: "Isn't she just to die?" asks Gorey. Yes, agrees his friend. She is without question to die.

Is it fair to say that a Gorey tale never has a happy ending? Another sigh. "Oh, I suppose it is, but I don't think it's particularly relevant. Some of my endings I would consider happy, but nobody else would." And to Marianne Moore, whom he scoops up into his lap, Gorey purrs softly: "You're such a tiny pusskins. You are such a love. Is there anything more heavenly than a silly little kitten?"

**to Sally A. Lodge, "PW Interviews Edward Gorey,"** *Publishers Weekly*, **November 26, 1982**

"My life is one morass of muddle. I don't throw things away. I just put them somewhere else. That means that the paths between my drawing board and the bed tend to vary from week to week.

"If I'm really concentrating I can put in about four to six hours drawing. After that it becomes exhausting work. I find it more difficult to write. I spend a great deal of time lying on my bed looking at the ceiling, hoping inspiration will come."

**to Fran Weil, "Mastery of Macabre Turns Gorey into Moneymaker,"** *Boston Herald American*, **March 27, 1975**

"I have given up considering happiness as relevant."

**to Alexander Theroux, "The Incredible Revenge of Edward Gorey,"** *Esquire*, **June 1974**

"(And a question of my own): Why did you answer these questions? It is, as a dear friend once wrote years ago in a context I no longer remember, 'a question perhaps only Philadelphia can answer.' "

**to Irene Reichbach, undated, unpublished questionnaire**

# Bibliography

Andrews, Peter. "Edward Gorey Onstage." *Horizon XX* (November 1977): 12–15.

Anonymous. "Proust Questionnaire." *Vanity Fair* (October 1997): 382.

Appleby, Stephen. "G Is for Gorey, Still Alive and Well." *Sunday Telegraph Magazine* (London): 52–55.

Baldauf, Scott. "Edward Gorey: Portrait of the Artist in Chilling Color." *The Christian Science Monitor* (October 31, 1996): 10–11.

Brassey, Tania. "Meet the Man Who Makes Children Do Terrible Things." *The Sunday Times* (London) (August 13, 1978): 13.

Brownstein, Elizabeth Smith. "Haunted Houses: Edward Gorey's House, Yarmouth Port, Massachusetts." *If This House Could Talk: Historic Homes, Extraordinary Americans.* (New York: Simon & Schuster, 1999): 218–223.

Cavett, Dick. "The Dick Cavett Show with Edward Gorey." WNET-TV, New York, (November 30, 1977).

Covert, Colin. "Edward Gorey Keeps it Eerie and Mysterious." *Detroit Free Press* (October 29, 1982): B1–2.

Cunningham, Bill. "Portrait of the Artist as a Furry Creature." *The New York Times* (January 11, 1978): C 13.

Dahlin, Robert. "Edward Gorey." *Conversations with Writers* (Detroit: Gale Research Company, 1977): 127–154.

Drozdowski, Ted. "The Welcome Guest." *The Boston Phoenix* (August 21, 1992): 7.

Dullea, Georgia. "Gorey Turns His Talent to Window Shudders." *The New York Times* (June 3, 1978): 16.

Dyer, Richard. "The Poison Penman." *The Boston Globe Magazine* (April 1, 1984): 8–9, 26, 28, 30, 32, 34, 36, 38, 44–45.

Filstrup, Jane Merrill. "Interview with Edward Gorey." *The Lion and the Unicorn, #1* (1978): 17–37.

———."The Cat Quotes of Edward Gorey." *Cats Magazine* (May 1978): 12–13, 28.

Fried, Kerry. "Playing Favorites." On *Amazon.com* (November 1998).

Gardner, Paul. "A Pain in the Neck." *New York Magazine* (September 19, 1977): 68–69.

Goolrick, Robert Cooke. "A Gorey Story." *New Times* (March 19, 1976): 54–58.

Green, Blake. "Welcome to Edward Gorey's Strange World." *New York Newsday* (April 14, 1994): B4–B5.

Gussow, Mel. "Gorey Goes Batty." *The New York Times Magazine* (October 16, 1977): 40–42, 70–71, 74–76.

———."At Home with Edward Gorey: A Little Blood Goes a Long Way." *The New York Times* (April 21, 1994): C1, C4.

Heald, Tim. "A Taste for the Macabre." *Sunday Telegraph Magazine* (London): 58–61, 66.

Heller, Steven. "Edward Gorey's Cover Story." *The National Post* (Canada) (January 6, 1999): B10–11.

Henwood, Simon. "Edward Gorey." *Purr* (London) (Spring 1995): 22–24.

Hodenfield, Jan. "And 'G' is for Gorey Who Here Tells His Story." *The New York Post* (January 10, 1973): 4, 73.

Hole, Judith, and Martha Teichner. "Out of the Inkwell." *CBS News Sunday Morning.* (April 4, 1997).

Judge, Diane. "That Oft–Passing, Silent Stranger Emerges as the Admirable Gorey." *New York Post* (October 22, 1978): 10.

Kare, Susan. "Gorey Story." *Choragos*. (October 31, 1974): 7.

Kissel, Howard. "The Revenge of Giselle . . . a Gorey Stage of Events." *Women's Wear Daily* (April 12, 1977): 20.

Kisselgoff, Anna. "The City Ballet Fan Extraordinaire." *The New York Times* (November 13, 1973): 50.

Kriegsman, Alan M. "The Glory of Being Gorey." *The Washington Post* (June 11, 1978): K1, K8, K9, reprinted as "A Frankenstein Person." *Sunday Record* (June 18, 1978): 13, 15.

———."An Artist Walks Off His Drawing Board." *International Herald Tribune* (June 22, 1978).

Landsberg, Mitchell "Illustrator is Gaining Wide Appeal." *Hartford Courant* (March 8, 1987).

Little, Craig. "Gorey." *Cape Cod Times Magazine* (October 30, 1977): 3–4, 19–20.

———."Authors and Artists: Edward Gorey, Profile I." *Cape Cod Life* vol. 1, no. 2 (1979): 30–32.

———."Edward Gorey Finds Designs in Fantasy." *Cape Cod Times* (December 24, 1979): 15.

Lodge, Sally A. "PW Interviews Edward Gorey." *Publishers Weekly* (November 26, 1982): 6–7.

Lydon, Christopher. "The Connection: Edward Gorey." WBUR, Boston, National Public Radio (November 26, 1998).

Mano, D. Keith. "Bio: Edward Gorey Inhabits an Odd World of Tiny Drawings, Fussy Cats and 'Doomed Enterprises'" *People* (New York: July 3, 1978): 70–73.

Martin, Jean. "The Mind's Eye: Writers Who Draw." *Drawing* (July–August 1980): 25–30.

McCrary, Michael. "G Is for Gorey." *Boston Rock* (October, 1995): 14–15.

McManus, Otile. "A Gorey Master of the Macabre." *The Boston Globe* (September 15, 1977): A8, A13.

McNamara, Mary. "Dead Letter Writer." *Los Angeles Times/Weekend* (October 29, 1998): 6, 8, 10.

Murphy, Cullen. "Gorey's World." *Bookletter* (February 16, 1976): 12–13.

Nocenti, Annie. "Writing the Black Doll: A Talk with Edward Gorey." *Scenario* (Spring 1998): 171–177.

Norris, Hoke. "Chicago: Critic at Large. The Skeletons in His Closet." *Book Week* (September 19, 1965): 6.

Petrucelli, Alan W. "A Niche of His Own: Edward Gorey." *Prime Time Cape Cod* (October, 1995): 8–10.

Pinsent, Ed. "A Gorey Encounter." *Speak* (Fall 1997): 42–47.

Ross, Clifford. "Interview with Edward Gorey." *The World of Edward Gorey*. (New York: Harry N. Abrams, 1996): 9–40.

Ross, Jean W. "CA Interview." *Contemporary Authors*, new revision series, vol. 30 (Detroit: Gale Research Inc., 1990): 164–166.

Rourke, Mary. "Strange Things Happen When Gorey Is Afoot." *The National Observer* (September 11, 1976): 18.

Ryan, Michael. "Bats, Cats, Dracula and the World of Gorey." *Us* (June 13, 1978): 69–71.

Segal, Lewis. "Edward Gorey's Danse Macabre." *Los Angeles Times Calendar* (March 2, 1986): 53.

Schalkhäuser, Helga. "Die Schaung-Schönen Gesichten des Edward Gorey." *Madame* (Munich; September 1984).

Schiff, Stephen. "Edward Gorey and the Tao of Nonsense." *The New Yorker* (November 9, 1992): 84–94.

Schoettler, Carl. "Gorey with a Dash of Red." *The Evening Sun* (May 19, 1978): B1.

Seligsohn, Leo. "A Merrily Sinister Life of His Own Design." *The Providence Sunday Journal* (June 25, 1978): E2.

Snyder, Camilla. "Boxed Inside the Macabre Is Sheer Whimsy." *Los Angeles Herald Examiner* (June 26, 1979): B1, B2.

Solod, Lisa. "Interview: Edward Gorey." *Boston Magazine* (September 1980), 77–78, 80, 82, 84, 86, 88–90, 92, 94, 96–97.

Stamm, Peter. "Schwarzmale." *Das Magazin* (Zurich, May 24, 1997): 38–42.

Stange, Eric. "At Home with Edward Gorey." *Boston Herald American* (November 22, 1981): 15.

Stevens, Carol. "An American Original." *Print* (January/February 1988): 49–63.

Streitfeld, David. "The Gorey Details." *The Washington Post* (September 14, 1997).

Syse, Glenna. "Blood and Gorey." *Sunday Sun-Times* (London) February 4, 1979.

Temin, Christine. "The Eccentric World of Edward Gorey." *The Boston Globe*.

Theroux, Alexander. "The Incredible Revenge of Edward Gorey." *Esquire* (June 1974): 110–111, 144, 146, 148.

———.*The Strange Case of Edward Gorey*. (Seattle: Fantagraphics Books, 2000).

Thomas, Phil. "A Writer First, Then an Artist." *Sunday Cape Cod Times* (January 15, 1984): 40.

Tobias, Tobi. "The Everynighters." *The New York State Theater Magazine, VIII* (May 1973): 13–15, 17.

———."Balletgorey." *Dance Magazine* (January 1974): 67–71.

Weil, Fran. "Mastery of Macabre Turns Gorey into Moneymaker." *Boston Herald American* (March 27, 1979): 18, 19.

Wheeler, Joan. "What's Halloween Without a Night of Gorey Entertainment?" *Day & Night* (October 20–October 28, 1999): 3.

Windmöller, Eva. "Heile Welt voller Schrecken." *Stern Magazin* (Hamburg, February 11, 1983): 64–69, 74.

Winer, Linda. "Gorey Story Behind 'Dracula' Settings." *Chicago Tribune* (February 4, 1979): VI, 3.

Wood, Tim. "Frightening Things About Life According to Edward Gorey." *A-Plus Magazine* (October 1995): 7–10.


ALSO SEE:

Gooch, Brad. *City Poet: The Life and Times of Frank O'Hara* (New York: Alfred A. Knopf, 1993).

Lurie, Alison. "V.R. Lang, A Memoir" *V.R Lang: Poems & Plays*. (New York: Random House, 1975): 1–71.

# Endnotes

## The City Ballet Fan Extraordinaire

1. The exuberant Patricia McBride joined the New York City Ballet in 1959 and was made a principal dancer in 1961. Balanchine made twenty-one roles for her. Famous for her partnership with Edward Villella, McBride danced with the NYCB until retiring in 1989.

2. *Liebeslieder Walzer* (1960), is a two-part ballet choreographed by Balanchine to Johannes Brahms's waltzes for piano duet and vocal quartet, *Liebeslieder*, *Op. 52* (1869), and *Neue Liebeslieder, Op. 65* (1874). In the first part, four couples, dressed in period ballroom costumes and dancing slippers, dance in various combinations in an elegant ballroom. In the second part, the women wear ballet dresses and point shoes, returning at the end in their original costumes to listen to a final waltz. Balanchine described the ballet by saying, "In the first act, it is the real people who are dancing. In the second act it is their souls."

3. These Balanchine ballets were frequently repeated staples of the NYCB repertory during the 1950s. Balanchine choreographed *Firebird*, to

Stravinsky's 1911 *Firebird Suite for Orchestra* (1910), for Maria Tallchief in 1949. Jerome Robbins collaborated, principally on the monsters' dance. Balanchine's one-act *Swan Lake* is set to music from Acts II and IV (the lakeside acts) of Tchaikovsky's full-length score of 1875–1876, plus a duet from his opera *Ondine*. It premiered in 1951, with Maria Tallchief as Odette. *Western Symphony* (1954), to traditional American tunes orchestrated by Hershy Kay, is one of Balanchine's tributes to his adopted country, a lighthearted romp for cowboys and dance-hall girls.

4. Balanchine's *Stars and Stripes* (1958), is both a tongue-in-cheek tribute to the United States and a celebration of pure, virtuoso classical dancing. Set to John Philip Sousa marches orchestrated by Hershy Kay, the ballet has been performed for such occasions as the inauguration of Nelson Rockefeller as governor of New York, tributes to Presidents John F. Kennedy and Lyndon B. Johnson, and the opening ceremonies of the New York State Theater at Lincoln Center.

# Balletgorey

TOBI TOBIAS, 1974

1. The Novice is the central figure in Jerome Robbins's ballet *The Cage*, to Stravinsky's *Concerto in D for String Orchestra, "Basler"* (1946), in which a tribe of predatory insect-women dispatch male intruders into their precinct. *The Cage* premiered by the New York City Ballet in 1951 with Nora Kaye (1920–1987), then a principal dancer in the company, known as an interpreter of dramatic roles, as the Novice. The "intestinal thing" is a skin-colored leotard appliquéd with irregular coils; the Novice's short hair is plastered to her head—Robbins's directive, according to a famous NYCB anecdote, after seeing Kaye leave a rehearsal with her hair still wet from a shower.

2. *Serenade*, to Tchaikovsky's *Serenade for Strings*, was choreographed by George Balanchine for his first gathering of American dancers,

American Ballet, and first performed in 1935, at the Adelphi Theater, New York. A signature work of the New York City Ballet, *Serenade* is one of Balanchine's purest and earliest statements of his simultaneous allegiance to the tradition of the Romantic ballet and to unabashed modernism. *Lilac Garden*, which has been described as "an essay in frustration," was choreographed by the British choreographer Antony Tudor, in 1938, to *Poème*, for solo violin and orchestra, by Ernest Chausson. First performed by the Ballet Club at the Mercury Theatre, London, it later entered the repertory of Ballet Theater and, still later, the New York City Ballet. Nora Kaye was celebrated for her interpretation of the principal role of Caroline.

3. Considered one of Balanchine's masterpieces, *Four Temperaments* (1946), is set to Paul Hindemith's *The Four Temperaments: Theme with Four Variations for String Orchestra and Piano* (1940), which was commissioned by Balanchine, an accomplished pianist, to play at home with friends. Choreographed for the opening program of Ballet Society, the forerunner of the New York City Ballet, *Four Temperaments* is one of Balanchine's earliest experiments with reinventing a classical vocabulary of steps in terms of a modernist, angular language of movement, directly paralleling the music's fusion of traditional structure and non-traditional harmonies.

4. *Agon* (1957) was a collaboration with Stravinsky, set to a specially composed score, *Agon* (1953–1956). Divided into sections named after French court dances, it is one of Balanchine's masterpieces, a radical reinvention and expansion of the inherited language of classical ballet. The pas de deux, made for Diana Adams and the Company's extraordinary African-American principal dancer Arthur Mitchell (later founder of the Dance Theater of Harlem), is among the ballet's most electrifying moments.

5. From 1953 until 1986, when he moved permanently to Cape Cod, Gorey lived at 36 East 38th Street, in a one-room apartment in an ornate 19th-century townhouse.

6. Suzanne Farrell (born 1945), was Balanchine's "muse" during her years as a principal dancer with the New York City Ballet, in the 1960s and

1970s. Farrell was known for her long line, long legs, and dynamic phrasing—a sense of movement being generated by intensifying a position almost to the point of losing balance. Balanchine made many important works for Farrell, including *Movements for Piano and Orchestra* (1963), to Stravinskys composition of the same name (1958–1959). She is the author of a memoir, *Holding on the Air*.

7. Before taking on administrative duties, Edward Bigelow (born 1918), danced with the New York City Ballet in the 1950s and early 1960s.

8. Known for her long limbs, elegant line, and her musicality, Diana Adams (1929–1993) was a principal dancer of the New York City Ballet from its earliest days in the late 1940s through the early 1960s. Among the many important roles Balanchine made for her, perhaps the most significant was the pas de deux in *Agon*.

9. *Prodigal Son*, to Serge Prokofiev's *Le Fils Prodigue, Op. 46* (1928–1929), is a dramatic, "primitivist" work choreographed by Balanchine in 1929 to open the last Paris season of the Ballets Russes of Serge Diaghilev. In 1950, it was revived for the New York City Ballet with Jerome Robbins as the Prodigal.

10. The neoclassical tour de force *Symphony in C*, to Georges Bizet's 1855 *Symphony No. 1 in C Major* (composed when Bizet was seventeen), was choreographed by Balanchine as *Le Palais de Cristal* for the Paris Opéra Ballet in 1947, after Stravinsky called his attention to the music. A year later, the ballet was performed for the first performance of the New York City Ballet, as *Symphony in C*, with simplified sets and costumes.

11. Allegra Kent was a principal dancer with the New York City Ballet in the 1950s and 1960s, known for her exceptionally articulate legs and feet, and her flexibility. Balanchine made several roles for her, including the protagonist of his staging of the dance-drama *Mahagonny* (now lost) at the City Center, with Lotte Lenya.

12. Gelsey Kirkland (born 1952) danced with the New York City Ballet from 1968 to 1974 (as a principal dancer from 1972–1974) before joining American Ballet Theater, where she danced until 1984. She has also

performed internationally as a guest artist. Ms. Kirkland is the author of a controversial memoir, *Dancing on My Grave*.

13. *The Tale of Genji*, by Lady Murasaki (Murasaki Shikubo), dates from the 11th century. An epic tale of intrigue, it is considered one of the first novels.

14. Ronald Firbank (1886–1926), English author and aesthete, known for his rather precious, exquisitely crafted novels. They include *Vainglory, Valmouth, Concerning the Eccentricities of Cardinal Pirelli,* and *Prancing Nigger.*

# Conversations with Writers: Edward Gorey
ROBERT DAHLIN, 1977

1. John Ciardi (1916–1986) taught at Harvard from 1946 through 1953, then at Rutgers. From the first publication of his poems in 1940, Ciardi was widely admired. Well known for his translations of Dante's *Inferno, Purgatorio*, and *Paradiso*, Ciardi also produced a series of enchanting books of verse for children, many of them illustrated by Gorey.

2. Merrill Moore (1903–1957) was known equally for his idiosyncratic adaptations of the sonnet form and his scholarly psychoanalytic texts. Gorey's endpapers for Moore's *Illegitimate Sonnets* (1950) are his first appearance in a commercial book. A sequence of "cartoons by Edward St. John Gorey" in Moore's *Case Record from a Sonnetorium* (1951) records Dr. Moore's successful treatment of the ailing Sonnet, in images of plump, bald men with sloping foreheads—the Sonnet crowned with laurel, Dr. Moore in lab coat and eyeglasses—the direct ancestors of Clavius Frederick Earbrass of *The Unstrung Harp.*

3. *L'Enfant de Paris* (1913) was directed by Léonce Perret for Pathé. Like *The Hapless Child*, it tells the story of a well-to-do Parisian officer who leaves his wife and child to go on duty in Morocco. Told he is missing

and presumed dead, his wife dies; their child is sent to live with an uncle. When the uncle is called to military service in Indochina—the film's sub-text is patriotic support of the French colonial presence—the child is sent to an orphanage. Like Charlotte Sophia, she steals away, ending up with a band of *apaches*—French thugs, not Native Americans. Unlike Gorey's *Hapless Child*, she is treated well, and after a complicated plot involving a ransom, she is happily reunited with her father.

4. This is a section of *Ivesiana* (1954). Balanchine choreographed the piece to a group of unrelated orchestral pieces by Charles Ives shortly before the composer's death in 1954. The second section, *The Unanswered Question*, to the 1906 composition of the same name, made for Allegra Kent, is the one described by Gorey.

5. Christian Morgenstern (1871–1914), German poet and humorist, wrote nonsense verse and macabre, pre-Dada poetry for adults, including *Gallows Songs* (1905), *Palmström* (1910), and *The Noise Mill* (1928).

6. Pamela Hansford-Johnson, *On Iniquity: Some Personal Reflections Arising Out of the Moors Murder Trial*, New York: Charles Scribner's Sons, 1967.

7. The controversial *Histoire d'O*, by the pseudonymous Pauline Réage (1907–1998), was first published in Paris in 1954, eventually reaching the U.S. in translation in 1965. It explicitly chronicles the progressive, willing debasement—both sexual and psychological—of a young woman, known only as O, who wishes to become the slave of her lover, René.

8. Samuel Foote (1720–1777) was a British playwright best known for his adaptations of French plays. He devised *The Great Panjandrum Himself*—not a poem, since it lacks rhyme or meter—as a challenge to the actor Charles Macklin,who boasted that he required only one hearing or reading of any text to be able to repeat it from memory. It reads: "So she went into the garden to cut a cabbage-leaf to make an apple-pie; and at the same time a great she-bear, coming down the street, pops its head into the shop. What! no soap? So he died, and she very imprudently married the Barber: and there were present the Picninnies, and the Joblillies, and the Garyulies, and the great

Panjandrum himself, with the little round button at top; and they all fell to playing catch-as-catch-can, till the gunpowder ran out at the heels of their boots."

9. Randolph Caldecott (1846–1886) illustrated a one shilling "Caldecott Picture Book" of *The Great Panjandrum*, with lively, economical line drawings (some colored) of sharply characterized figures in Regency costumes.

10. The first of Gorey's several exhibitions at James Graham and Sons was held in 1974. The prestigious New York gallery specializes mainly in nineteenth- and twentieth-century American art.

11. *Allegra Kent's Water Beauty Book*, with an introduction by Edward Villella and exercise photographs by Hank O'Neal. New York: St. Martin's Press, 1976.

12. Edmund Wilson's article "The Albums of Edward Gorey" in *The New Yorker*, December 26, 1959, was the first important critical notice of Gorey's work. Gorey later illustrated Wilson's children's thriller *The Rats of Rutland Grange*, first published in *Esquire* in 1961 and in book form, in 1974, by the Gotham Book Mart.

13. Gorey's silent film script *The Black Doll* hinges on the fate of a Priceless Ritual Object excavated from the ruins of the central Asian city of Gulb (or Blug) by the American archaeologist Professor Horace Bedsock in an expedition financed by Maximilian Gloat. Various villains, including the Fiend, "an insane international master-criminal," and the Comtesse de Macache Bézef, hereditary high priestess of the ancient cult of the Bear That Dances, plot to steal the object. The professor's daughter Daisy and her fiancé, Seth Irongate, "a young man of independent means," are, of course, on the opposing side. The script was published in *Scenario*, Spring 1998.

14. In *V. R. Lang: A Memoir*, Gorey's close friend the novelist Alison Lurie, a Radcliffe student when he and O'Hara were at Harvard, recalls that the Poets' Theater of Cambridge was founded in the fall of 1950. Its yearly prospectus stated that "several of New England's outstanding

poets joined forces with a group of younger writers in an effort to revive poetic drama." The "outstanding poets" were Richard Wilbur, John Ciardi, and Richard Eberhart. The "younger writers" included John Ashbery, Edward Gorey, Donald Hall, Frank O'Hara, Lyon Phelps, and V. R. Lang, all associated with Harvard. Except for Lang, whose work had already been accepted by *Poetry* and *The Chicago Review*, most had published only in the *Harvard Advocate*. At first, the Poets' Theater was perceived as a radical outpost of what Lurie calls the "furthest avant-garde." After 1952, when the original group graduated and left Cambridge for New York and Europe, the theater allied itself with the Harvard faculty.

## The Dick Cavett Show with Edward Gorey

DICK CAVETT, 1977

1. Cavett probably found this frequently stated and frequently quoted observation in Alexander Theroux's interview with Gorey, "The Incredible Revenge of Edward Gorey," *Esquire*, 1974: "I ask him, awkwardly, as I recall it, *why* he thinks stark violence and horror and terror are the uncompromising focus of his work. 'I write about everyday life,' comes Gorey's simple reply, out of a shadow."

2. Gustave Doré (1832–1883), celebrated French draughtsman, engraver, and illustrator,. was a master of wood engraving, known for the romantic intensity of his illustrations for the Bible and other classics.

3. Max Ernst (1891–1976), German-born painter, long resident in France and the United States, was a pioneer of French Surrealism. In 1972, he saw an exhibition of Gorey's work at the Gotham Book Mart Gallery, which included drawings for *The West Wing*, and was extremely interested and enthusiastic.

4. Sir John Tenniel (1820–1914), attended the Royal Academy, but was disgusted by the low quality of teaching. He exhibited his paintings

from the age of sixteen, and received a number of prestigious commissions, including a fresco for the House of Lords. Principally a political cartoonist (with a strong Tory bent) he produced the main political cartoon for *Punch* from 1850 to 1901. He is best known for his illustrations for Lewis Carroll's *Alice's Adventures in Wonderland*, 1865, and *Through the Looking Glass*, 1872.

5. Dalziel Brothers was a famous British firm of engravers, founded by George and Edward Dalziel in 1839, later joined by their brothers John, in 1852, and Thomas, in 1860. Thomas and Edward also made book illustrations of their own, as well as engraving those of other artists.

6. Gorey's will established a charitable trust to support organizations that benefit what trustee Andreas Brown describes as "the full spectrum of living entities." Three organizations named specifically by Gorey as eligible to receive funding are the Cape Cod chapter of The Animal Rescue League of Boston, the Xerces Society of Portland, Oregon, dedicated to the study and conservation of invertebrates, their environment and habitat, and the Bat Conservation International Foundation of Austin, Texas.

7. The 1931 silent film *Dracula*, directed by Tod Browning, starred Bela Lugosi as the elegant vampire-count.


# An Interview with Edward St. John Gorey at the Gotham Book Mart

JANE MERRILL FILSTRUP, 1978

1. Charles Perrault (1628–1703), French Academician and writer, is best known for his collection of fairy tales, *Contes de fées*, which includes versions of Hop-o'-my-thumb, Little Red Riding Hood, Puss in Boots, Blue-Beard, and Cinderella.

2. Bruno Bettelheim (1903–1990), *The Uses of Enchantment: The Meaning and Importance of Fairy Tales*, New York: Knopf, 1976.

3. *The Young Visiters or, Mr. Salteena's Plan* was written by Daisy Ashford at the age of nine and first published in 1919, when the author, then an adult, discovered it "with other childhood mementoes among the effects of her lately deceased mother." A thrilling romantic tale, it contains such memorable lines as "I will put some red ruge on my face, said Ethel, because I am very pale owing to the drains in this house."

4. Amanda M'Kittrick Ros (1860–1939), author not only of *Irene Iddesleigh*, 1897, but also of the novels *Helen Huddleson, Donald Dudley, the Bastard Critic,* and *Delina Delaney;* and *Fumes of Formation*, a collection of poems, all published in her lifetime.

5. The six "Lucia" novels, *Queen Lucia, Lucia in London, Miss Mapp, Mapp and Lucia, The Worshipful Lucia*, and *Trouble for Lucia*, and one short story, "The Male Impersonator," are rapier-edged comedies of manners that recount the story of Mrs. Emmeline Lucas (Lucia) of Riseholme, her arch-enemy, Miss Elizabeth Mapp of Tilling, and their friends, rivals, and neighbors among the British upper middle class. E. F. Benson (1867–1940) began the series in the 1920s and continued them until his death. The omnibus edition referred to by Gorey is *Make Way for Lucia*, a collection of all six books (New York: Thomas Y. Crowell, 1977). In the 1986 Harper and Row reprint, and editor's note to "The Male Impersonator" thanks "Edward Gorey, America's chief Luciaphile," for bringing the story, previously published in 1929 in an edition of 530 copies to his attention.

6. Charles Cros (1842–1882) was a visionary French poet and pioneer of color photography.

7. Alphonse Allais (1854 or '55–1905), French humorist, poet, and playwright, was admired by the Surrealists.

8. Paul Eluard (1895–1952), French Surrealist poet, was, with André Breton, a founder of the movement. He was particularly close to the Surrealist painters and sculptors, as well as to Picasso, and wrote frequently about their art.

9. See Fried, note 1, page 272.

# The Mind's Eye: Writers Who Draw

JEAN MARTIN, 1980

1. The first of Gorey's several exhibitions at Graham Gallery, New York, was held in 1974, the same year that his major retrospective exhibition, *Phantasmagorey: The Work of Edward Gorey*, organized and with a catalogue by Clifford Ross, was seen at the Sterling Memorial Library, Yale University, New Haven. The retrospective traveled in the U.S. for three years. Gorey's previous exhibitions were held at the California College of Arts and Crafts, Oakland, in 1965; at the Minnesota Institute of Arts, Minneapolis, in 1968; at the University of Texas, Academic Center, Austin, at the San Francisco Public Library, in 1971; and at Pennsylvania State University, Pattee Library, University Park, in 1973. Since 1970, there have been annual exhibitions of Gorey's work at the Gotham Book Mart Gallery, New York. Gorey's first British exhibition was held at Francis Kyle Gallery, London, in 1979.

2. Gorey's list is distinctly eclectic, including as it does Georges de La Tour (1593–1652), the French master of meticulous candle-lit dramas; Pierro della Francesca (1415/20-1492), the Umbrian painter of such uncanny geometrically lucid masterpieces as the frescos of the Story of the True Cross in San Francesco, Arezzo; and Paolo Uccello (1397-1475), the Florentine virtuoso of perspective, best known for his three large commemorative paintings of the Battle of San Romano, with their rigid rows of armored knights and "carousel horses." Many painters on Gorey's list require no introduction, such as the French modernists, Henri Matisse (1869–1954), Edouard Vuillard (1868–1940), and Pierre Bonnard (1867-1947), all celebrated for their formal and coloristic innovations. Others are less familiar to the general public: Balthus (born 1908), the French painter known for his sexually charged, oddly static images of nude young women; Francis Bacon (1909–1992), the British chronicler of existential angst in a homosexual underworld, and Charles Burchfield (1893–1967), the American watercolor painter of stylized, ecstatically animated landscape motifs.

3. Edward Lear (1812–1888) is the renowned author of such classic non-sense verses as *The Dong with the Luminous Nose* and *The Jumblies*, both illustrated by Gorey, along with countless limericks. His bestiary includes the Pobble Who Has No Toes, the Runcible Cat with the Crimson Whiskers, and the immortal Owl and the Pussycat. British illustrators Edward Bawden (1903–1989) and Edward Ardizzone (1900–1979), both well known as painters, were official war artists during World War II. Bawden was particularly admired for his linocuts and lithographs, published by the Curwen Press over more than sixty years. Prints such as the series *Six London Markets* are strongly graphic, with stylized figures elegantly deployed in simplified dramatic spaces. Ardizzone's first illustrations were for Sheridan Lefanu's *Through a Glass Darkly* (1929). Later, he wrote and illustrated a series of children's books, the "Tim" series, beginning with *Little Tim and the Brave Sea Captain* in 1935. He wrote and illustrated more than twenty books for children, and illustrated more than 150 books by other authors, including Charles Dickens, Mark Twain, Robert Louis Stevenson, and Dylan Thomas. His work is characterized by a vigorous, supple line and refreshingly unsentimental imagery.

# Edward Gorey

LISA SOLOD, 1980

1. Gorey told Alexander Theroux in "The Incredible Revenge of Edward Gorey," *Esquire*, June 1974, that he worked for Adlai Stevenson in 1952, in Boston: "'But,' Gorey says, 'I became unstrung by it all. ' " Theroux continues: "Politics bore Gorey. (Here, however, he pauses, flings a leg over his chair, and suddenly adds, 'Nixon'—the sigh comes from his foot-sole—'works me up terribly.')"
2. Francis W. Parker, a private, progressive school.

3. The English novelist and illustrator William Makepeace Thackeray (1811–1863) first published his great social satire *Vanity Fair: A Novel Without a Hero* in monthly installments in 1847. The definitive edition, incorporating changes Thackeray believed to be improvements, appeared in 1864.

4. Patrick White (1912–1990), British-born Australian novelist, playwright, short-story writer, poet, and memoirist; winner of the Nobel Prize in Literature in 1973. His books are both highly esteemed and regarded as immensely difficult because of their dense layers of symbols, myths, and allegories, their complex structures and themes, and what one critic called their "choking thickets of imagery."

5. Theroux reports, in his 1974 *Esquire* interview, that "when packed off to church, [Gorey] claims he used to 'throw up.'"


# The Poison Penman

RICHARD DYER, 1984

1. Eve Arden (1908–1990) was a deep-voiced actress and comedienne, best known for *Our Miss Brooks,* on radio and TV in the late 1940s and 1950s. Her film roles included appearances in *Mildred Pierce, Stage Door,* and *The Women.*

2. Other anagrammatic Gorey pseudonyms include Drew Dogyear, Wardore Edgy, Raddory Gewe, Aedwyrd Goré, Garrod Weedy, Madame Groeda Weyrd, and Dedge Yarrow. Eduard Blutig and O. Müde are translations into German of "Edward Gorey" and "Ogdred Weary," respectively.

3. Among these Harvard and Radcliffe alumni, some of the most distinguished in the literary world include: Alison Lurie (born 1926), the author of a series of sharply honed satiric novels about academics and writers. Lurie's first published work was a 1956 memoir of her (and Gorey's) friend, the poet V. R. Lang; her best-known novel is probably

*The War Between the Tates*. George Plimpton (born 1927), known as a flamboyant journalist, was a founding editor of *The Paris Review*, which he continues to edit. Donald Hall (born 1928), whose poems have appeared in *Times Literary Supplement, The New Yorker,* and *Partisan Review*, was the first poetry editor of *The Paris Review*. He is the author of numerous children's books, some illustrated by Gorey, of an autobiography and a study of Henry Moore. John Ashbery (born 1927) is a distinguished poet known also as the editor of books of poetry and, especially, as a perceptive art critic. Kenneth Koch (born 1925), poet, playwright, and short-story writer, has been a professor at Columbia University since 1959. Between 1958 and 1966, he directed the Poetry Workshop at the New School for Social Research.

4. Frank O'Hara (1926–1966), poet, playwright, art critic, curator, and friend of artists and poets, was a legendary figure of the New York art and literary worlds of the 1950s and early 1960s. As a critic, he wrote perceptively about the work of Helen Frankenthaler, Larry Rivers, Jane Freilicher, Grace Hartigan, Fairfield Porter, and other members of the "Second Generation New York School," and often posed for them. The Tibor de Nagy Gallery, where they showed their work also published modest booklets of poetry by O'Hara and his colleagues, illustrated by gallery artists. The gallery was associated with the New York Artists Theater, the successor to the Poets' Theater, in Cambridge, Massachusetts, which O'Hara helped found when he was at Harvard. His play *Try! Try!*, first produced by the Poets' Theater in 1951, with sets by Gorey, was performed in a second version by the Artists Theater in 1953, with sets by Hartigan. The author of a monograph on Jackson Pollock (New York: Braziller, 1959), O'Hara is probably best known for his trenchant, vernacular poems, originally published as *Meditations in an Emergency* (1956), *Second Avenue* (1960), and *Lunch Poems* (1964).

5. The Old Howard was a celebrated Boston burlesque house, located on Washington Street roughly where Government Center is now.

6. Gorey made this trip, his only venture outside the United States, in 1975. He traveled to Fair Isle, the Orkneys, the Shetlands, the Outer Hebrides, and Loch Ness. He commented: "I did not see the monster, to my great regret—the great disappointment of my life, probably."

7. *Gorey Stories* was performed from January 27 to February 5, 1978, at the WPA Theater, Off-Broadway, then brought to Broadway, to the Booth Theater. Gorey was fond of saying that *Gorey Stories* lasted only one night—October 30, 1978—but he rarely added that the premiere took place during a New York newspaper strike, which essentially meant that there were no reviews. A review read on the radio was very positive.

8. "Les Trocks" is an immensely popular all-male ballet company, the apotheosis of the camp sensibility, who perform the classic repertory with a combination of sheer determination, technical fortitude, and deadpan hilarity.

9. See note 14, page 253.

10. The British illustrator Ernest Howard Shepard (1879–1976) is equally well known for his memorable drawings for the A. A. Milne Winnie-the-Pooh books.


# An American Original

CAROL STEVENS, 1988


1. Leonard Baskin (1922–2000), sculptor and graphic artist, and Ben Shahn (1898–1969), painter and documentary photographer, were highly regarded artists, especially in the 1950s, known for their stylized, often socially conscious images. Their spiky, spontaneous drawings, frequently used for commercial purposes, exerted considerable influence on the more intellectually ambitious advertising of the period.

2. John Wulp directed the Playwrights' Horizons Theater School from 1983 to 1990. He now teaches and paints "on an island in Maine."

3. *The Mikado*, with sets, costumes, and a poster by Gorey, was performed at Carnegie Mellon's Kresge Theater, April 14–30, 1983. *Tinned Lettuce,* 1985, for which Gorey also designed sets and costumes, was the first musical review written entirely by Gorey.

## Edward Gorey and the Tao of Nonsense
STEPHEN SCHIFF, 1992

1. Samuel Beckett. *Beginning to End,* New York: Gotham Book Mart, 1988, and T. S. Eliot, *Old Possum's Book of Practical Cats,* New York: Harcourt Brace Jovanovich, 1982.
2. Louis Feuillade (1873–1924), artistic director of Gaumont Fils, the company that, along with Pathé, pioneered the French silent film, from one-reelers to full-length narratives. He directed about 800 comedies, farces, dramas, and thrillers, most very short, most now lost. See note 1, page 266.
3. From the early 'teens through the 1930s, gatherings at the London and Oxfordshire homes of Lady Ottoline Bentinck Morrell (1872–1938) and her husband, Philip Morrell, a Liberal Member of Parliament, were legendary. Their friends included philosopher Bertrand Russell; writers W. B. Yeats, D. H. Lawrence, T. S. Eliot, Lytton Strachey, E. M. Forster, Siegfried Sassoon, and Virginia Woolf; painters Augustus John, Stanley Spencer, and Duncan Grant—among many other luminaries.
4. *The Secret Garden* is Frances Hodgson Burnett's 1911 children's book about a pair of cousins who live in a vast, gloomy Yorkshire manor house replete with endless corridors, grounds with walled gardens, and cheerful, no-nonsense local types.
5. In his 1977 interview with Gorey for *Esquire*, Alexander Theroux described him as "seriously attracted to Taoism" and "more than well acquainted with Chinese translator Arthur Waley's *Three Ways of Thought in Ancient China* and the extracts of Chuang Tzu."

6. For Firbank, see note 14, page 253. Evelyn Waugh (1903–1966), author of mordant, satirical novels including *Vile Bodies, The Loved One,* and *Brideshead Revisited*, is well known to American readers. Ivy Compton-Burnett (1884–1969) produced such lean, dialogue-driven novels as *Pastors and Masters, Daughters and Sons,* and *Elders and Betters*, about claustrophobic family circles. C(ecil) Day-Lewis (1904–1972) first attracted attention as an engagé left-wing poet; after his break with the left, he was acclaimed for his personal, formally rigorous lyricism. From 1968 until his death, he was Poet Laureate of England. Henry Green (1905–1973), the pseudonym of Henry Vincent Yorke, a manu-facturer and novelist, wrote wry satires with such laconic titles as *Living, Party-Going, Nothing,* and *Loving*; W. H. Auden called him "the best English novelist alive." Gorey did the cover for the Anchor Book edition of *Loving*.

7. See note 12, page 255.

8. The American writer William Burroughs (1914–1997) is best known for *Naked Lunch* (1959), a stream-of-consciousness series of tales of his life as a drug addict. A controversial writer even after conquering his addiction, he was championed by Norman Mailer and Mary McCarthy. Brion Gysin (1916–1986) was an English painter, inventor, writer, and recording artist.

# Edward Gorey

SIMON HENWOOD, 1995

1. Louis Feuillade (1873–1924). Among his most acclaimed films are *Les Fantômas*, five films made between April 1913 and May 1914 which were the first highly successful crime series. The protagonist is an anar-chist masquerading as a correct bourgeois gentleman, a doubling that is compounded in the series by Fantômas's opponent, Police Inspector

Juve. Throughout the series, the two reverse roles, Juve disguising himself as a criminal and Fantômas pretending to be a detective. *Les Vampires* (1915–16), starring Musidora, was the first serial thriller, followed by *Judex* (1917), another exploration of a double life; *Tih-Minh* (1918–19), Feuillade's venture into exoticism; *Barrabas* (1919); and *La Nouvelle Mission de Judex* (1920).

2. Mircea Eliade (1907–1986), Romanian-born historian of myth and religion, professor at the University of Chicago 1956 to 1985, novelist, and man of letters, was best known for studies of comparative religion, including *The Myth of Eternal Return, The Sacred and the Profane*, and the three-volume *History of Religious Ideas*.

3. *The Marriage of Cadmos and Harmony*, New York: Knopf, 1993, is the translation of Roberto Calasso's *Le Nozze di Cadmo e Armonia* (Milan: Adelphi, 1988).

4. *On Iniquity*; see note 6, page 254.

5. Brad Gooch, *City Poet: The Life and Times of Frank O'Hara*, New York: Knopf, 1993, includes substantial information about Gorey's Harvard years.

6. Mikio Naruse (1905–1969), along with Yasujiro Ozu, was one of the great masters of the genre known as "shomin-geki," which deals with realistic problems of life in the lower middle class. His work ranged from short slapstick comedies to the serious domestic dramas for which he is admired. His best-known films include *Three Sisters with Maiden Hearts* (1935), *Repast* (1951), and *Late Chrysanthemums* (1954), which Gorey discusses. Naruse's last film was *Scattered Clouds* (1967).

7. Yasujiro Ozu (1903–1963), another master of "shomin-geki," was a cameraman and then director of silent films in the late 1920s. Many of his early films have vanished, but like his surviving ones, they remain legendary. Among the most acclaimed are *I Was Born, But . . .* (1932) and *A Story of Floating Weeds* (1934). *The Only Son* (1936) was Ozu's first sound film. His later works include *Tokyo Story* (1953) and *An Autumn Afternoon* (1962).

8. *The Tale of Genji*, by Lady Murasaki (Murasaki Shikubo), was translated by Arthur Waley in the 1920s and '30s in six volumes. A more recent translation by Edward Seidensticker dates from the 1970s.

## Edward Gorey: Portrait of the Artist in Chilling Color
SCOTT BALDAUF, 1996

1. Carl Theodor Dreyer (1889–1968) began his career as a journalist, scriptwriter, and writer of intertitles for silent movies; he made his first film in 1919. He is best known for *The Passion of Joan of Arc* (1927), with the stage actress Maria Falconetti, a "documentary" of the trial of the Maid of Orléans, told largely through close-ups of expressive faces, and for the fantasy *Vampyr* (1932).

2. Gorey wrote, directed, and designed the sets and costumes for both productions. *Crazed Teacups* was performed in Provincetown, Massachusetts in 1992; *Blithering Christmas* was performed in Bourne, Massachusetts, in 1993.

3. V. S. Pritchett, *The Gentle Barbarian: The Life and Work of Turgenev*, 1977.

## The Gorey Details
DAVID STREITFELD, 1997

1. Gilbert Canaan (1884–1955), British barrister, critic, translator, playwright, poet, and novelist. Canaan abandoned law for a literary career after publishing a translation of Romain Rolland's *Jean Christophe* in 1907. Ten years later he suffered a breakdown and was institutionalized for the rest of his life.

2. Charles Morgan (1894–1958), author of, among many other novels, *The Empty Room, The Flashing Stream,* and *The Gunroom.*


# Writing *The Black Doll*: A Talk with Edward Gorey

ANNIE NOCENTI, 1998

1. See note 2, page 265, and note 1, page 266.
2. See note 13, page 255.
3. The adjective "*gemütlich*," defined by Cassell's German-English Dictionary as "cozy, snug, comfortable, genial, friendly, pleasant," becomes "*ungemütlich*": "uncomfortable, cheerless, unpleasant."
4. "The MacGuffin" was Alfred Hitchcock's term for the—necessarily arbitrary—motivating object or event in a thriller.
5. Charlotte Sophia, in fact, is the tragic heroine of *The Hapless Child.* She called her doll Hortense.
6. Charlie Chan, the fictional Chinese detective, was the hero of a series of movies made in the 1930s and 1940s, and later of a British TV series. Chan was played by a series of non-Asian actors, beginning with Warner Oland, followed by Sidney Toller and J. Carrol Naish. Dr. Fu Manchu, "the Yellow Peril in a single man," was created by the British novelist Sax Rohmer (1883–1959), the pseudonym of Arthur Henry Ward, in a series of novels beginning in 1913. The first Fu Manchu movie was made in 1932, with Boris Karloff in the role of the evil master criminal, with new versions appearing in the 1960s.
7. *The Perils of Pauline* (1914), starring Pearl White, was the first of the "cliffhanger" serials. Miss White, who did many of her own stunts, later starred in a series of similar epics, all named for their heroines, who, like Pauline, narrowly escaped frightful dangers week after week.

8. D. W. Griffith, actor, writer, and director, was the leading American director of silent films and a pioneer of feature-length movies. After making countless one- and two-reelers for Biograph, between 1908 and 1913, Griffith made *The Birth of a Nation* in 1914, the most successful silent film ever made. In 1919, he banded together with Charlie Chaplin, Douglas Fairbanks, and Mary Pickford to form their own production company, United Artists. Griffith went on to make such legendary silent epics as *Intolerance* (1916), *Broken Blossoms* (1918), and *Way Down East* (1920), many of them with his long-suffering heroine, Lillian Gish.

9. The French director Georges Franju (1912–1987), a co-founder of the Cinémathèque Française, made *Les Yeux Sans Visage* (*Eyes Without a Face*) in 1959. A great admirer of Feuillade, he directed a new version of *Judex*, turning the principal character into a kind of Robin Hood cum terrorist. Schüftan was also Franju's cameraman for his first feature film, *La Tête Contre le Murs* (*The Keepers*), 1958.

10. Jacques Tourneur (1904–1977) came to the U.S. from Paris at the age of ten, when his father, Maurice, came to direct films for Eclair Studios in Fort Lee, New Jersey. After returning to Europe as his father's assistant, Tourneur directed his own first feature in 1931. He worked in Hollywood after 1939, and later in television as well, directing films such as *The Flame and the Arrow*, with Burt Lancaster, and *Way of a Gaucho*, with Rory Calhoun. Montague Rhodes James (1862–1936) was an eminent Biblical scholar and art historian, who wrote extensively about the Apocrypha and the Apocalypse, edited an edition of the New Testament, and several books on ancient manuscripts. He also was a prolific writer of ghost stories and published several collections in his lifetime.

11. *That Obscure Object of Desire* (1975) was the Spanish-born Surrealist filmmaker Luis Buñuel's last film. Buñuel (1900–1983) always intended to use two very different actresses in the same role, to convey the different facets of the character, but in fact cast the dual role twice, first with Isabelle Adjani and Maria Schneider and finally with Angela Molina and Carole Bouquet. Buñuel's oeuvre ranges from *Un Chien Andalou*

(1929), made in collaboration with Salvador Dalí, to *Belle de Jour* (1967), and *The Discreet Charm of the Bourgeoisie* (1972).

12.  Alain Resnais (born 1922), the film director whose aesthetic most closely approximates that of the writers, such as Nathalie Sarraut, associated with the affectless "*nouveau roman.*" Resnais is best known for *Hiroshima, Mon Amour* and *Last Year at Marienbad*.

13.  Henri-Georges Clouzot (1907–1977) was a French director known for his tense suspense dramas, such as *Diabolique* (1954), with Simone Signoret, an unsettling tale of rivalry and conspiracy, and *The Wages of Fear* (1963), with Yves Montand, the terrifying story of desperate men who risk their lives driving trucks loaded with explosives over primitive roads. *La Prisonnière*, which Gorey mentions, was made in 1968. Clouzot also made a remarkable film about Picasso at work, *The Mystery of Picasso* (1955).

14.  Von Trier is best known to English-speaking audiences for *Breaking the Waves* and *Dancer in the Dark*. Girod's *The Infernal Trio* (1974) featured Michel Piccoli as an impeccably correct, but murderous lawyer, aided by his two lovers, a pair of sisters.

15.  Jean-Pierre Mocky (born 1929), screenplay writer, adapter of novels, actor, and director, little known outside of France, worked several times with the cameraman Eugen Schüftan, whom Gorey admired.

# The Connection

CHRISTOPHER LYDON, 1998

1.  A monumental unfinished novel by Austrian-born writer Robert Musil (1880–1942), *The Man Without Qualities* (1930–43) is a sophisticated, witty vision of the disappearing world of the Austro-Hungarian Empire.

2.  Elizabeth Sewell, *The Field of Nonsense*, Folcroft Library Edition, 1952; reprinted 1973.

# Playing Favorites

KERRY FRIED, 1998

1. Raymond Queneau (1903–1976) was a poet and novelist associated in the 1920s with the Surrealists in Paris, and a contributor of poems and "Surrealist texts" to *La Révolution Surréaliste*. He also wrote critical studies of James Joyce and Joan Miró. He sometimes used the pseudonym "Sally Mara." The books recommended by Gorey are: (translated from the French) *Exercises in Style, A Hard Winter, Pierrot, Between Blue and Blue: a sort of novel, The Bark Tree, The Flight of Icarus, The Sunday of Life, The Skin of Dreams, We Always Treat Women Too Well, Zazie in the Metro, Odile, The Last Days, St. Glinglin,* and *Children of Clay.*

2. The five Mennyms books are about a family of life-size rag dolls living in a house in England, pretending to be human and in constant fear of their secrets being exposed. First published in Great Britain, then in the United States by Greenwillow Books, between 1993 and 1996. They are *The Mennyms, Mennyms in the Wilderness, Mennyms Under Siege, Mennyms Alone,* and *Mennyms Alive.*

3. Charles Williams (1886–1945) was an English novelist, author of *The Place of the Lion, Shadows of Ecstasy,* and *All Hallows' Eve.* E. W. H. Meyerstein (1889–1952) was an English scholar, novelist, poet, dramatist, and music critic. His novels include *Robin Wastraw, Tom Tallcon, Phoebe Thirsk*, and the *Life of Chatterton.*

4. Robert Musil (1880–1942). Gorey refers to *The Man Without Qualities*, translated from the German by Sophie Wilkins and Burton Pike, New York: A. A. Knopf, 1995, and *Diaries 1899–1941*, original German edited by Adolf Frise, English edition selected, translated, and annotated by Philip Payne, edited by Mark Mirsky, New York: Basic Books, 1998.

# Edward Gorey's Cover Story

STEVEN HELLER, 1999

1. Gorey is referring to his covers for Joseph Conrad's *Victory* and Henri Alain-Fournier's *The Wanderer*. *The American Tourist* remains unidentified.
2. Mikhail Iurevich Lermontov (1814–1841), celebrated Russian poet and writer.
3. Charles M. Doughty, *Travels in Arabia Deserta*. (In the original article, this appears as *The Arabian Deserter*.)
4. Andrew Lang (1844–1912) was the British translator of traditional French tales and author of a dozen collections of fairy tales, each titled for the color of its cover—*The Blue Fairy Book, The Green Fairy Book, The Pink Fairy Book,* and so on—published between 1895 and 1910.
5. George Herriman, who created Krazy Kat, illustrated one edition of *archy and mehitabel*, by Don Marquis (1878–1937), a collection of free-verse poems about life "from the under side," composed by archy, a cockroach inhabited by the soul of a *vers libre* bard—all lower case because archy can't work the shift mechanism. Mehitabel is his friend, the alley cat whose motto is *"toujours gai."*

# Acknowledgments

My thanks to the Trustees of the Estate of Edward Gorey for their generous cooperation with this undertaking and to all the writers and publishers who agreed to make work available for republication. I am deeply indebted to Andreas Brown, of the Gotham Book Mart, who originally conceived of this project, and whose enthusiasm, guidance, support, and tireless efforts to unearth useful material vastly enriched this book. I am also grateful to Gina Guy, for her help in locating drawings by Gorey. My thanks, too, for their essential contributions, to Sheila Samton, Joel Honig, Matthew Samton, Sandi Slone, and John Griefen.

—KAREN WILKIN

# Permissions Acknowledgments

"And 'G' Is for Gorey Who Here Tells His Story," by Jan Hodenfield, is reprinted with permission from the *New York Post*. Copyright © 1973, NYP Holdings, Inc.

"The City Ballet Fan Extraordinaire," by Anna Kisselgoff, is reprinted by permission of *The New York Times*.

"Balletgorey," by Tobi Tobias, is reprinted by permission of the author.

"Conversations with Writers: Edward Gorey," first appeared in *Conversations with Writers, Volume 1* by Robert Dahlin. Copyright © 1977 by the Gale Research Company. Reprinted by permission of The Gale Group.

"The Dick Cavett Show with Edward Gorey" is printed by permission of Daphne Productions, Inc.

"The Cat Quotes of Edward Gorey," by Jane Merrill Filstrup, is reprinted by permission of *Cats Magazine*.

"An Interview with Edward St. John Gorey at the Gotham Book Mart," by Jane Merrill Filstrup, first appeared in *The Lion and the Unicorn,* Number 1, 1978, and is reprinted by permission of *The Lion and the Unicorn*.

"The Mind's Eye: Writers Who Draw," by Jean Martin, was first published in *Drawing,* July–August, 1980.

"Edward Gorey," by Lisa Solod is reprinted by permission of *Boston Magazine*.

"The Poison Penman," by Richard Dyer, is reprinted with the permission of the *Boston Globe Magazine*. Copyright © 1984 by Globe Newspaper Co. (MA).

"An American Original," by Carol Stevens Kner, is reprinted by permission of the author.

"Edward Gorey and the Tao of Nonsense," by Stephen Schiff, is reprinted by permission of the author.

"Edward Gorey," by Simon Henwood, first appeared in *Purr* (London), Spring, 1995.

"Edward Gorey: Portrait of the Artist in Chilling Color," by Scott Baldauf, first appeared in *The Christian Science Monitor* on October 31, 1996, and is reproduced with permission. Copyright © 1996 by the Christian Science Publishing Society. All rights reserved.

"The Gorey Details," by David Streitfeld, is reprinted by permission of *The Washington Post*. Copyright © 1997, *The Washington Post*.

"Edward Gorey: Proust Questionnaire" is reprinted by permission. Copyright © 1997 Condé Nast Publications Inc. Originally published in *Vanity Fair*. All rights reserved.

"A Gorey Encounter," by Ed Pinsent, is reprinted by permission of the author.

"Writing the Black Doll: A Talk with Edward Gorey," by Annie Nocenti, is reprinted by permission of the author.

"The Connection," by Christopher Lydon, is the edited transcript of a radio interview broadcast November 26, 1998, on "The Connection," a production of WBUR, Boston, hosted by Christopher Lydon. Printed by permission.

"Playing Favorites," by Kerry Fried, is reprinted by permission of the author.

"Edward Gorey's Cover Story," by Steven Heller, is reprinted by permission of the author.

# Index

*Note: Book titles refer to works by Gorey unless otherwise specified.*
*Names followed by an asterisk (\*) refer to fictitious characters.*